The Prepper's Freeze Drying Cookbook

Delicious and Nutritious Recipes for Survival and Preparedness

Cody Stroud

Table of Contents

Introduction

We have a wide range of options available to us when it comes to preserving food, whether for personal consumption at home or in a professional food setting. These options include cooling, freezing, canning, sugaring, salting, and vacuum packaging. Preservation experts are continually researching new techniques to expand our range of options. It's crucial to prioritize safe food preservation methods that have been developed through centuries of trial and error. This ensures that stored food remains of good quality and cleanliness. Fortunately, with the proper instructions and resources, food can be preserved in any situation. Food preservation involves preparing food for safe, long-term storage, whether for personal use, professional kitchens, or direct sale to customers. Preserved food remains safe and delicious to consume in the future since preservation techniques limit bacterial growth and spoilage. There are three primary reasons why food preservation is crucial:

1. Pathogenic bacteria - Pathogenic bacteria such as E. coli, Salmonella, and other harmful pathogens can cause food spoilage during long-term storage. Bacteria need heat, moisture, and time to reproduce quickly in food, but preservation methods limit one or more of these factors, halting their proliferation.

2. Maintaining high food quality - Over time, food quality deteriorates due to spoilage. While moderate spoilage may not render food unsafe to eat, it can significantly alter its taste, texture, and appearance. Proper food preservation can help maintain some of these characteristics and preserve the nutritional value of specific foods.

3. Saving money - Food can be expensive, whether at home or in a food business. Ideally, one should avoid buying more food

than they can consume. However, safe preservation techniques allow for the storage of vegetables, fruits, meat, and other foods beyond their expected expiration date, eliminating the need to dispose of them. Although some food preservation techniques may be challenging to master, once learned, a sense of accomplishment and pride can be felt. Additionally, a better understanding of food hygiene issues and best practices can be gained since many preservation techniques require precision and care to ensure food safety. This book will discuss the best method for preserving food: freeze-drying. Let's get started without delay.

Freeze Drying Basics

Freeze drying is a method of food preservation that removes all moisture from a specific food without affecting its taste. Agricultural products are dried to reduce the amount of water in them, and freeze-drying is a preservation technique that involves freezing the sample material below its glass transition temperature, causing frozen water to dissolve as the process pressure and temperature are reduced. This modern dehydration technique removes moisture efficiently while causing minor structural deformation in the product. Due to the low process enthalpy, it is a less severe thermal process that minimally degrades heat-sensitive compounds while protecting thermolabile constituents. Freeze-drying requires a two-step process that starts with freezing the food, which then undergoes a vacuum cycle. This cycle converts all ice gems formed during freezing into a fume, which is removed from the food, making it safe for consumption without losing its tone or taste. Freeze-drying has been used for centuries, as seen in the Incan empire, which developed Chuo, a freeze-dried potato that could sustain their massive armies for years. Chuos are still eaten in the Andes today and can be rehydrated to make freeze-dried mashed potatoes or ground into flour that can thicken stews and soups. Freeze-drying removes about 99% of the water content from food items, giving them a longer shelf life than dehydrated food, and rehydrates easily and quickly, making it ideal for storing food for an extended period. Freeze-dried food should be consumed within four months of opening, but when packaged correctly in airtight and vacuum-sealed mylar bags, it can last long, even in a cupboard. This method of food preservation is preferred by NASA when packing food for astronauts, and preppers like it for preserving meats and other cooked foods for their bunkers and go bags because it keeps them fresh indefinitely. However, it is not recommended for backpackers and climbers, as it can contribute to dehydration in the body and cause gastrointestinal issues. In summary, freeze-drying is a modern dehydration technique that removes moisture efficiently while preserving the taste and quality of food, making it a useful method for preserving food for an extended period.

Science Behind Freeze-Drying

The structure undergoes less shrinkage and deformation when frozen. A vacuum pump can generate a vacuum by reducing the pressure below the triple point of water, while monitoring the pressure using sensors like a capacitance manometer. Latent heat of sublimation is provided by heating plates. Using a refrigerated condenser, the vacuum pump extracts sublimated vapors from the process chamber and condenses them into ice. The rate of drying slows down because the ice/sublimation front moves backward when ice molecules sublime.

Low pressure or vacuum reduces the rate of diffusion. The volume reduction of a porous structure is negligible compared to other drying methods when ice is removed. During the drying process, evaporated vapors can be recovered by condensing them in a refrigerated condenser. The microscopic porous structure aids reconstitution by efficiently regaining maximum water, improving product quality, allowing for the recovery of crispy texture, and shortening the rehydration cycle time.

Freeze-dried products containing 2% MC have a shelf life of about two days. The end products of the process are of high quality and do not require refrigeration. If resistance occurs at the mouth of the pore, pore blockage kinetic theory can be investigated to improve the quality of the dried products. The drying process should maximize component retention (such as ascorbic acid, nutrients, and vitamins), preserve nutritional and sensory values, and reduce processing time and capital costs. Freeze-drying is used for solid raw materials like fruits, vegetables, and meat, as well as for liquid raw materials like homogeneous solutions. The freeze-drying process is completed in three major stages, with no pre-treatment required for the raw materials.

In the plate, blast, immersion, or liquid blast freezing method, water in a sample of food is frozen below its eutectic temperature. Successful freezing occurs when 95 percent of the water is converted to ice. Freezing affects the distribution of pore size. The optimal freezing rate must be chosen because it affects the drying rate and the final product quality. The eutectic point can be determined using thermal analysis techniques such as cryo-microscopy, differential scanning calorimetry, and time versus temperature curve methodologies. The freezing rate governs crystal growth and ice morphology. Slow freezing results in larger crystals, a porous structure, and an increased drying rate, which damages the product's tissues and reduces rehydration efficiency.

Accelerated freezing produces small ice crystals that promote intense nucleation while permitting easy reconstitution and rapid drying.

Initial Drying

The process chamber pressure is lower (13.5 270Pa absolute) than the ice vapor pressure in the sample material to sublime ice. Conduction and radiation through the lower and upper plates provide latent sublimation heat. As a result of initial drying or ice sublimation, a dry layer forms on the top surface of the sample product. Diffusion through this partial dry layer or heat movement through the frozen and dry layers determines the drying rate. A refrigerated condenser condenses diffused vapors, and a vacuum pump is used to remove non-condensable gases. This is the longest stage of the freeze-drying process.

During initial drying, a temperature range of -20 to +20 is maintained. Heat transfer can only occur through conduction or radiation because convection lacks its medium due to the absence of air. The product is heated to a temperature below its glass transition temperature. In initial drying, the condenser temperature should be lower than the product temperature. The maximum heat should be less than its eutectic temperature, which raises the pressure difference between the condenser and the product. Heat transfer stops when the product and shelf temperatures become the same, resulting in lower system pressure and condenser temperature values due to no evaporated load. The end of initial drying can be accurately determined using comparative pressure measurement methods.

Freeze-drying preserves the nutritional value, heat-sensitive compounds, color, shape, texture, size, aroma, and flavor of agricultural products. The ongoing development of freeze-drying, as well as future aspects, make its application very feasible. The primary process parameters vary depending on the chemistry of the subjected product. Freeze-drying is an ancient technique that has evolved and continues to improve. However, freeze-drying has a high process and fixed cost. The freeze dryer freezes the product's water before applying the latent sublimation heat to sublimate the frozen water and then increasing the heat to remove any remaining water.

Freeze Drying with a Freeze Dryer Machine

If you're planning a large-scale freeze-drying empire or simply want to try freeze-drying, one of these machines might be worth investing in. A freeze-drying machine will undoubtedly be a worthwhile investment if you own a farm or a fruit farm. It is important to note that if you need to prepare food for storage quickly, having a freeze dryer in your home will not save you much time. If you want something quick and efficient, other methods are preferable. Overloading the trays and containers of a freeze dryer is not permitted. The drying time will vary between one day for thin slices of meat and fruits and three days for thicker and larger chunks of food.

To get into the deep end of freeze-drying, you must first understand that three steps must occur for a satisfying freeze-dried product to be produced. You can buy a freeze-drying machine or rig something together if you're daring by following YouTube tutorials. Numerous resources are available to teach you how to set up a vacuum chamber in your home.

The first step in creating a DIY home freeze-drying rig is to freeze. You'll need a heavy-duty freezer that can withstand temperatures as low as -30°F or even lower. As previously stated, you can also flash freeze the items with liquid nitrogen for this stage. Second, you'll need an airtight vacuum-sealed chamber and a vacuum pump to extract moisture from your food. This second stage is known as initial drying or sublimation. Finally, there is desorption, also known as secondary drying. Attach a thermostat and a heater to the rig so that you can gradually add heat to the chamber to draw the remaining moisture out. This step is required so that you can adjust the temperature inside the chamber to repeat the sublimation process. A humidity sensor is also needed to determine whether all of the moisture has been removed from your food items.

Armed with this knowledge, you should now ask yourself a few questions before beginning your freeze-drying adventure. What are you going to do with it? Will it only be used for camping or backpacking? Do you buy bulk and plan to freeze-dry cooked items for your family's meals? Or are you a doomsday prepper preparing for the end of the world or nuclear fallout?

Whatever your reason, even a home freeze-drying machine will be an expensive purchase. It is highly preferable to consider your reasons. You don't want to spend a thousand dollars on equipment that will only be used once and collect dust in your basement or garage. Additionally, these machines are large and heavy, taking up much space in your kitchen.

One of the best ways to preserve your groceries or surplus garden harvest is to freeze-dry them. Sublimation removes water from food by converting it from a solid to a vapor or gas. Freeze drying is one of the best ways to preserve food because it retains almost all nutritional value.

Canning and dehydrating food changes the flavor and color and reduces the nutritional content by half. Freeze-dried foods can be stored in the refrigerator, pantry, or cellar for up to 25 years. They're small and lightweight, making them ideal for quick camping meals or an emergency food supply. Most homeowners can access a home freezer and dry ice if they do not have a freeze-dryer.

Preparation of Freeze-Dried Food

Before freeze-drying your food, select the freshest options. The food should then be chopped into small pieces or bits to remove moisture. Cooked meals, on the other hand, can be frozen entirely.

If you can afford it, a freeze-dryer is an excellent option because it is explicitly designed for freeze-drying. There are numerous dryers to choose from, so make sure you get an affordable one. The advantage of these dryers is that they come with various trays for different meals.

Follow the procedures below to freeze-dry your goods. Remember to test your meals before storing them if you use this method:

- Place your meals in the trays, ensuring they do not exceed the tray's height.
- Place the trays in the dryer after closing the doors (Some models have two doors).
- Freeze the food between -40 and -50 degrees Fahrenheit.
- Allow 24 hours for the procedure to be completed.
- After they're done, place the food in Mylar bags and seal them.

How Does a Home Freeze Dryer Work?

The following is an excerpt from "The Good, the Bad, and the Ugly of Home Freeze Drying":

- First, you get a sturdy freezer (Harvest Right units can reach -30°F or lower).
- Second, you pair it with an airtight chamber capable of maintaining a vacuum (no oxygen) at all times.
- Finally, you connect a vacuum pump powerful enough to remove zebra stripes.
- Install a heater and thermostat to cycle the temperature up and down for many hours, repeating the sublimation process.
- Fifth, connect a humidity sensor to confirm that the water has evaporated and the cycle is complete.

Many goods, such as dairy products, whole meals (hot dishes, cream-based soups, etc.), and leftovers, cannot be preserved conventionally but can be frozen at home. Fruits, vegetables, meats, and seafood can also be preserved.

Using a Machine to Freeze Dry

Freeze-drying food with a machine is about as simple as it gets. You wash the food you intend to save and cut them into smaller pieces. When the food is ready, place it on the machine's tray, turn it on, and use the machine as the manufacturer directs.

When the food has finished drying, place it in a fixed plastic pack and store it. Although drying food varieties with a machine is quick and easy, it is quite expensive.

You can expect to spend a significant amount of money. If you want to take the easier route and use this strategy to protect your food, be prepared to contribute.

People who are new to freeze-drying food benefit from having a home freezer. This is an even better option if you have a deep freezer. However, your standard home freezer will continue to work.

1. Place the food on a tray or dish after being spread out.
2. Place the tray in the freezer to freeze the food at the coldest temperature possible.
3. Allow the food to freeze for 2–3 weeks or until entirely freeze-dried.
4. After completing the procedure, store it in an airtight storage bag in your freezer or pantry.

Freeze Drying without a Machine

Freeze-drying with a machine is simple, but doing it without a machine isn't too tricky.

The primary difference between using a machine and not one is the amount of time the interaction takes. If you dry food without a machine, you should prepare it as you usually would before securing it with another method.

When the food is finished, place it on an air-drying rack so the air can completely circle it.

Place the plate in a deep cooler and leave it there. The food will immediately freeze. The food will become dry in a matter of weeks.

You will notice that the food has wholly dried by removing one piece. If the food doesn't change color as it defrosts, you'll know the interaction is finished.

How to Freeze-Dry Food with Dry Ice

Use protective equipment for this process because dry ice can burn your skin.

Place the food in a freezer bag and freeze it with dry ice. If you leave it open, the escaping air could cause your bag to explode. Pile a lot of dry ice on top of the freezer bag and leave it for 24 hours to dry. After 24 hours, the container or freezer will be filled with carbon dioxide, so do this in a well-ventilated area. Carbon dioxide inhalation in confined spaces can be fatal. If successful, frozen food must be stored in vacuum-sealed airtight containers with no moisture allowed to enter the bag.

It saves time to use dry ice instead of frozen food. This is because dry ice quickly evaporates moisture from the meal. Fill freezer bags with the food. Place the bags in the fridge. Freeze the bags for 24 hours, completely wrapped in dry ice. Remove and store the bags after they have entirely freeze-dried.

Items that are ideal for freezing with dry ice:

- Broth: Take a handful and use it for cooking or flavoring.
- Citrus juice can be used in beverages, seasonings, and dressings.
- Coffee/Tea: Use cool beverages like iced coffee and iced tea without diluting them.

- Herbs: Combine 2 cups fresh herbs and 1 cup water in a blender until smooth, then pour into trays. Frozen herbs are convenient for incorporating into cooked or pureed foods such as soups, sauces, and marinades.

Yogurt can be stored in the freezer for 2 to 3 months. You can blend it into a smoothie as a creamier alternative to ice.

Freeze-Drying Food Using Liquid Nitrogen

If you want to freeze dry items at home, another method that will undoubtedly come up when you search the internet is liquid nitrogen. Of course, liquid nitrogen quickly freezes food when it comes into contact with it. Liquid nitrogen, at -320°F, will freeze anything it comes into contact with and should be handled cautiously. Often, liquid nitrogen will be used as a faster way to bring the food to a temperature below freezing before a vacuum pump can extract all of the moisture from the food. If you don't have a drying machine, you can still flash freeze your food before storing it in the freezer with liquid nitrogen.

Instructions for Storing Freeze-Dried Food

Currently, your food options are freeze-dried. What would be a fantastic next step for you? When food sources have finished drying, place them in a plastic sack or compartment that seals.

There is no compelling reason to keep the items in the refrigerator or cooler. If all else is equal, store them in a cool place with temperatures no higher than 75°F.

This could be a root cellar, storage room, or bureau in many homes.

Food security did not appear to be this simple for many years, but we are fortunate. You can dry your food for long-term storage in just a few hours.

You can also store it for an extended period without any special requirements. You may have considered freeze-drying if you're looking for a simple way to save food.

Freezing - The Most Effective Method To Freeze Dry Food

Freezing food is a simple process that requires no special equipment, making it ideal for beginners. Prepare your vegetables by blanching or cooking them before freezing. This process inhibits enzyme activity while maintaining high quality. Blanching involves heating your vegetables and immersing them in cold water to stop cooking. Blanching time in boiling water is expected to be three minutes.

Freeze-drying appears to be an excellent method of food preservation, leading you to believe it is extremely perplexing. In any case, freeze-drying food has been around for a long time. It is straightforward and can be refined with or without a machine.

Vacuum sealing frozen products prevents ice crystal formation and can increase the shelf life of frozen items by three to five times. Non-vacuum-sealed items are rarely placed in the freezer. On the other hand, fruits can be frozen "as is" or added with a bit of sugar or antioxidants to help extend storage life and slow discoloration. If you want to freeze fruits and vegetables for longterm storage, consider freezing them on a cookie sheet and then vacuum-sealing them. This helps prevent ice crystal formation, which can increase the storage life of your frozen fruits and vegetables by up to 5 times.

Freezing is one of the most straightforward and convenient methods of food preservation and one of the oldest, along with dehydration. Before the invention of modern home appliances, communities in the far north or near mountain ranges discovered that food did not spoil in freezing temperatures. The power of cold temperatures gave rise to ice boxes (literally, metal boxes stuffed with ice), which eventually evolved into the refrigeration we have today.

Because freezing lowers the temperature of food, micro-organisms can no longer function, and enzymes act at a much slower rate. It's worth noting that I didn't say it "kills" the microorganisms; they're still there, just not moving. Enzymes will also be present and working much slower, but they will still function, implying that decay will occur much more slowly. Because spoilage elements are still present, once an item thaws, it begins to spoil quickly.

The goal of freezing food is not only to keep it fresher for longer but also to preserve its quality. With this in mind, you should place your food in the freezer with as little air as possible. Food deteriorates due to a leak when exposed to air from outside or within the container.

You can freeze anything you can process in a jar and even more, but deciding which method to use requires weighing the benefits and drawbacks of freezing food. Freezing is ideal for seafood, berries, and other perishable produce (like broccoli). Freezing preserves much of the nutritional value, color, and texture of foods, but there are drawbacks to be aware of. A freezer has limited space; you cannot choose to freeze everything. And, unlike other methods, freezing necessitates defrosting and, in some cases, cooking. It's also difficult to transport unless you have a portable freezer.

Frozen foods, on the other hand, have a shelf life of 3 to 1 year when properly stored. When the temperature of your freezer fluctuates (due to a malfunction, power outage, or being left open for too long), the quality of the frozen items inside can suffer. If there is a prolonged rise in temperature, it is critical to check all frozen items (especially meat) to ensure that they are still frozen. If the item has completely thawed, you should prepare it within the next few days or refreeze it. Label these items with the date and the word "refrozen."

Frozen foods can last for months if properly stored. Because germs cannot develop when food is frozen, food stored in the freezer can be consumed for almost indefinite periods. However, its quality will quickly deteriorate and become unappealing, so most frozen foods should be consumed within a few months to a year.

- To freeze food securely, set the freezer to a temperature between -18°C and -22°C. Place food in airtight containers or freezer bags before freezing. Meat is especially prone to freezer burn and becomes unusable if not properly packaged.
- Items should be frozen only before their best-before or use-by dates.
- Never refreeze defrosted food because it allows germs to grow between thawings.
- Consume it right away or refrigerate it for up to 24 hours.
- Defrost the freezer frequently to avoid ice accumulation. You should be able to store frozen items in the refrigerator for a few hours while the freezer defrosts.
- Foods should be labeled with the date they were frozen. You can check the expiration date to see if you should eat the food before it spoils. To determine the shelf life of frozen foods, use our online guide.

The Freezing Procedure

Freezing isn't rocket science; you've almost certainly done it before, but there are ways to do it better. This is how.

1. Clean Out Your Freezer

If you want to maximize your freezer and use your freezing skills to the fullest, you must first overhaul your freezer. Empty it, assess everything inside, and decide which items are old and/or will be used in a reasonable amount of time. Be honest: are you going to use everything in there? It's also fine, to begin with, an empty freezer so you can fill it with purpose. After you've emptied it, thoroughly clean it, and make sure it has a thermometer, either built into the unit or one you add.

2. Select and Prep Your Ingredients

Select the best and most fresh ingredients you can find. Fruit should be at its peak of flavor, vegetables should be young, and meats should be of the highest possible quality. Wash everything thoroughly but do not soak anything because retained water expands as the item freezes, breaking food tissues and cell walls and reducing quality. As needed, pre-treat. Freeze 101.

3. **Divide Your Frozen Items Into Portions**

You can portion things however you want if you have the proper vessels to place them in. This allows you to freeze quantities based on how much you want to eat or serve.

Refrigerate animal proteins until ready to cut, and work in small batches as you package them to avoid contamination and quality loss.

Cut fruits and vegetables to your liking and place them in a single layer on a parchment paperlined tray to freeze. Freeze liquid ingredients in pint or quart containers or heavy-duty resealable plastic bags. If you're freezing in a bag, seal it and place it on a rimmed baking sheet to freeze; once frozen, stack the bags to store.

4. **Put Labels On Your Packages**

On each package, label your items and include the date frozen. If you want, include words like "spicy," "sugar-free," or "contains nuts."

5. **Change Out Your Frozen Foods**

Place new freezer items in the back of the freezer and older items in the front. This policy, known as "FIFO" (first in, first out), ensures that older food is used first, reducing waste. Make a raw protein section on the bottom or separate it from other items in the freezer. This reduces the risk of cross-contamination if a meat container breaks or leaks.

However, unlike smoking or curing, freezing does not kill bacteria that can cause food to spoil. Because freezing only stops or slows bacterial growth, spoilage can still occur if your items are not appropriately frozen. To avoid this, food must be frozen quickly and kept at a temperature below 0°F at all times.

By keeping your freezer temperature at or below 0°F, you can not only stop the growth of bacteria that can cause spoilage but also reduce changes in the texture, nutritional value, and flavor of your foods.

Things To Consider Before Freezing Your Food

Arrange items in your freezer, so there is enough space between them for cold air to circulate, allowing for an even freeze—only stack items on top of each other when they are completely frozen. At the same time, avoid opening and closing your freezer multiple times daily. The constant temperature fluctuation will cause the items inside the freezer to thaw and freeze repeatedly. Even minor changes in the freezer will cause the smaller ice crystals to grow larger over time, causing further damage to the meat's cell structure and, in the long run, a softer and mushier texture. Temperature changes will also cause water to seep out of the meat, making it less juicy and healthier.

When freezing cooked meat, including the sauce, gravy, or marinade in the bag. This can also help to prevent moisture loss and freezer burn. Before storing it in the freezer, you should also allow pre-cooked food to cool to room temperature. Still, hot food takes a lot more energy to cool down and freeze, raising your electricity bill. Allowing your items to cool to room temperature slows the freezing process and helps maintain their quality.

Some loose food items, such as fruits and vegetables and lower-priced meat, can be tray-packed.

Tray-packed items are first arranged in a tray to be quickly frozen so that individual pieces do not touch one another or in one thin layer that is easily broken up when frozen. Afterward, the items are collected and placed in a smaller container or bag for easier access. Berries, broccoli, chopped chicken, chicken wings, patties, and nuggets are all examples of tray-packable foods.

If you don't already have a vacuum sealer, you don't need to buy one if you're only freezing a few items for your home. It is important to note that this is not vacuum packing because you will be unable to remove all of the air from the bag. To do so, fill a large bowl halfway with water and place your meat in a resealable freezer bag. Zip it almost up until you have about a quarter-inch left open. Submerge the bag slowly in the water, slowly pulling down until all the air is pushed out and only the tip left open is above the water.

Butter and margarine can also be frozen when cut and separated by smaller pieces of parchment or baking paper. While the butter or margarine is still cool, cut it into smaller flat squares—place parchment paper between the layers and freeze.

Try to portion the items according to the number of servings you intend to use. This will keep your food from spoiling due to repeated thawing.

Because water expands when frozen, your food will do the same. To prevent leakage, give your meats some wiggle room when packing them in resealable plastic bags. Before putting your items in the fridge, ensure they are correctly labeled. This will save you significant time searching for the right items. It also reduces the time the freezer is left open while you search.

Defrost or thaw food in the refrigerator, with a tray or plate underneath to catch the juices. Food should not be left to thaw in a warm place because it will spoil. Consider the enzymes responsible for its breakdown when freezing food. These enzymes are responsible for hastening the ripening or maturing of plants and the breakdown of cellular structures in meats. If these reactions are allowed to continue, the food's color, flavor, and texture will change. To avoid this, many people blanch the food quickly or add ascorbic acid to prevent browning.

Blanching is the process of quickly immersing food in boiling water for 30 seconds to a minute, followed by rapid cooling in an ice bath. This is mainly done with vegetables, stopping and inactivating the enzymes while also killing any micro-organisms on the surface. Blanching your vegetables allows you to store them for longer periods and takes up less space in your freezer.

Chemical compounds such as ascorbic acid, also known as Vitamin C, can prevent browning on fruits typically eaten raw and thus cannot be blanched. Lemon juice can be substituted for vitamin C if it is unavailable.

The most common issue people face when it comes to meat is rancidity. Freezing meat that will be cooked in a few weeks is fine, especially if it has already been vacuum-packed and frozen. However, if you plan to store fresh meats from the butcher for an extended period, it is best to trim the excess fat and place them in an airtight wrap or a vacuum-sealed plastic bag. This extra step will also help prevent freezer burn, which is damage to meat or other food caused by moisture loss and exposure to air. While the meat is still safe to eat, it may develop dark or gray spots, and the surface may resemble leather. On the other hand, fruits and vegetables will have their water content converted into ice crystals, shriveling and drying out.

Another factor to consider is the food's texture. When water freezes, it expands, so when you freeze food, the cell walls break down or rupture as the water inside them freezes. When the food has finally thawed, it will have a softer or mushy texture. Because of their higher water content, some vegetables and fruits exhibit this effect more than meat. As a result, if you find frozen fruit chunks in your freezer, serving them while they are still partially frozen is best.

Cooking the food beforehand softens the cell walls, reducing the adverse effects. Food that is quickly frozen can produce better results. According to research, the larger the ice crystals, the longer it takes for the food to freeze. As a result, it will cause more cell damage. However, rapidly freezing the food results in smaller ice crystals, which reduces cell damage. This is why flash freezing is often used to preserve the quality of freshly caught seafood for the journey to your table. This is also done to all types of meat typically sold chilled in supermarkets, thawed ahead of time for the shopper's convenience.

Fortunately, this method is not limited to large manufacturers. You can also do rapid freezing at home without any special equipment. All you need is a freezer; fortunately, the freezer in your refrigerator will suffice most of the time.

Maintaining Quality When Freezing

You can take steps to ensure higher quality results when freezing, such as pre-treating produce, blanching, and preventing discoloration and freezer burn. Some items, for example, must be pre-treated to maintain their structure in cold temperatures. Similarly, most vegetables should be blanched before freezing, which can be accomplished by lightly steaming or boiling them. Blanching inhibits enzyme activity.

Some fruits, such as cut apples, darken when exposed to air. Apply one of three options to the fruit before freezing to prevent discoloration: lemon juice, salt water (2 teaspoons salt to 2 cups water), or a salt-vinegar solution (1 tablespoon salt + 1 tablespoon vinegar and 2 quarts water). This is especially important when working with lighter-colored fruits.

Freezer burn is another food-quality concern when it comes to freezing. Dehydration in frozen food is referred to as freezer burn. It may be found on the edges of frozen items where there is air exposure. It is not harmful but can affect the product's texture and flavor. Limiting the air to which a product is exposed by removing as much air as possible from the bags (vacuum sealing is ideal) or leaving only 12 inches of headspace in containers. Wrapping items tightly in aluminum foil or plastic wrap and taping them well also helps avoid freezer burn.

Tools and Equipment

Some of these are required (such as the freezer!) while others are optional.

Containers

Heavy-duty resealable plastic bags, plastic pint or quart containers, or other tougher plastic containers can be used. Many use "deli cups" from restaurant supply stores. It all depends on the size of the items you're storing and how efficiently these storage containers use the freezer space. Use heavy-duty foil and wrap it in plastic wrap to prevent tearing. And, as much as I love using glass for preservation projects, it is brittle.

Pack meat in appropriate containers. Different foods necessitate slightly different containers. Use caution when using large containers because they will cause the items to freeze slowly, which is counterintuitive to our goal. As a general rule, freezer containers should be food grade, moisture proof, waterproof, durable, odorless, leakproof, and designed for the freezer. This means they should not crack or become brittle after prolonged use in the freezer.

Freezer-grade containers include plastic resealable freezer bags, rigid and resealable metal, glass, or plastic containers, and flexible or soft plastic/silicone containers. Carefully read the back labels of any containers you intend to purchase. They should be clearly labeled as freezer-safe. Most manufacturers would also include temperature limits for their products. Choose items that can withstand temperatures as low as 0°F.

Rigid containers hold liquids, soft foods, and easily broken down foods. The straight and hard sides make it simple to remove the food with a wet towel applied to the outside surface of the container. Most of them are also meant to nest or stack on top of one another. Metal and plastic are the most common materials used to make these containers. glass is another option; however, it should be noted that it has been tested for freezer use. Regular glass containers, such as canning jars can easily crack when temperatures drop below freezing. When using rigid containers, ensure the lids are tightly closed and airtight. If they are not, use freezer tape (tape designed for temperatures below freezing). Masking tapes should not be used because they may not adhere correctly.

The resealable plastic freezer bags and wraps that are widely available in stores are the most commonly used. Heavy-duty aluminum foil can also be used in a pinch. To avoid puncturing, keep them away from sharp objects and corners inside the freezer – using cardboard dividers in the freezer can protect the plastic wraps and aluminum foils. These bags are ideal for drier foods such as chops and steaks, as well as raw meat, fish, poultry, fruits, and vegetables.

Another container that has recently gained popularity on social media is the resealable silicone container, which can also be used as a freezer container. Because it is a hybrid of rigid, softer, more flexible wraps and bags, many people prefer it. Additionally, it is more durable than plastic freezer bags and is an environmentally friendly alternative to freezer bags.

Freezer

There are two types of freezers: upright and chest. Most of us are probably used to upright freezers. It is either a refrigerator/freezer combination or a stand-alone freezer. There are numerous size, style, and appearance variations. Because they are taller rather than wider, the uprights take up less space. However, these freezers are typically much smaller (especially when attached to a refrigerator) and lose cold air quickly when opened. If you need to do some serious freezing, chest freezers are ideal. They are larger and remain cold even when the door is opened because cool air tends to sink to the bottom. They do require more floor space. Whichever you choose, place it away from heat sources, such as your oven, and leave 2 to 4 inches between the back of the unit and the wall to allow for good airflow, which means the appliance won't have to work as hard to keep the temperature cold.

Ice-Cube Tray Made of Silicone

Although there is a long list of things that can be frozen in ice cube trays, you can also use these trays to portion out items that have a big impact in small doses, like lemon juice. Silicone ice cube trays are preferred because they make it easier to remove items from these trays.

Bags and Vacuum Sealer

A vacuum sealer machine removes all of the air from a specially designed bag; the bag conforms to a frozen item, cutting out oxygen. Simple sealers cost between $70 and $1,000 for commercial-grade sous vide sealers. Vacuum sealers are ideal for expensive items like meats and proteins because they ensure that as little air as possible comes into contact with the item, resulting in less freezer burn. This is also an excellent method for preparing single portions of large batch items; you can maximize storage space by eliminating unused space.

Freezing Meat at Home

If you intend to freeze fresh meats at home, turn on the freezer and keep the temperature inside well below freezing – around -10°F or even lower – for a few hours ahead of time.

Meat that will be used within a week or so can be frozen in its original packaging; however, meat that will be stored for an extended period must be properly packaged and sealed. When storing meats for an ample time, keep them away from air and in an airtight or vacuum-sealed freezer bag to avoid freezer burn.

When working with fresh meats you have just brought home from the store, and you must work quickly and efficiently so that the meat does not have enough time to thaw while working thoroughly. Keep your countertop, hands, utensils, and equipment clean to avoid contamination. To prevent food poisoning, you must exercise extreme caution when handling raw poultry. Also, to keep your family safe, remember to clean and disinfect afterward.

To maintain the quality of the meat, the freezer temperature must be kept below 0°F even after the initial freeze is complete. Allowing food to be stored in a freezer at temperatures above 0°F may result in spoilage and shorter shelf life. Food that has been frozen should be kept frozen.

Place it in the coldest part of the freezer, usually against the walls. Take care not to crowd the area. Cramming your freezer with unfrozen food all at once will result in a slow freeze.

Red Meat

If you are a hunter or butcher, freezing your red meats may be the simplest and quickest thing you can do with them when you have a large quantity and have yet to find the time or the right recipe to make your summer sausage.

Most butchers and delis will gladly freeze your meat for you. It's ideal if you don't want to cook your meat immediately. Put them in the freezer when you get home.

Red meat can be frozen relatively easily. Simply keep them away from moisture and air to maintain their quality. Remove any excess fat and, if possible, all of the bones. It may arrive wrapped in plain butcher paper when you buy fresh meat from the butcher or the store. Meats wrapped in butcher paper or other paper wraps in the store cannot be relied on to prevent freezer burn.

If you don't intend to use them within a week of purchasing them, take them out and rewrap them in a freezer bag or a freezer-safe container. If you don't intend to remove the butcher paper, simply wrap them in a freezer-grade wrap or place them in a freezer-proof bag. Items purchased vacuum sealed and frozen, on the other hand, would require rewrapping. It's fine to refreeze them when you get home.

Furthermore, if you are storing or packing multiple individual cuts of meat in one package or container, place freezer paper or baking paper in between each piece to prevent them from freezing together for easier thawing. Tray packing smaller chunks of meat or cut pieces of poultry is also an option. Tray packing means freezing your meats in a baking tray, arranged, so they do not touch. Cover the tray with freezer-safe plastic wrap and place in the freezer until completely frozen. These can then be placed in smaller, more compact containers for easier storage.

Salted meats such as hams and luncheon meats should not be stored in the freezer even if they are already cured. You will notice that the salt in the cured meats causes your meat to go rancid faster. For other cured meats, such as hotdogs and luncheon meats, freezing temperatures cause the emulsions inside to break down and leak, causing the meat to "weep."

Lower temperatures will cause cooked meat to dry out much faster than raw meat. It is therefore strongly advised to store it in the sauce in which it was cooked. Submerge or coat your meats in gravy before sealing them in a bag or container. After thawing, your meats will retain their freshness while also becoming more flavorful from having had more time to absorb the sauce. However, remember that meats frozen in sauces or marinades will last much less time than fresh raw meat. Try to finish them within three months.

Poultry

When selecting poultry that is best for freezing, choose whole, fresh, and unblemished birds. To ensure freshness, choose plump and odorless ones. You can certainly buy poultry that has already been butchered, but it is well worth your time to learn how to cut up your poultry correctly. It is far easier than it appears and far easier than butchering beef or pork.

Pull and separate the legs and wings from the body before separating the thigh from the drumstick. Split the ribcage in half, separating the back from the breast. If desired, cut the breast in half to make smaller servings.

When selecting the right poultry to freeze, consider how you intend to cook it. Choose more flavorful birds if you want to cook stews. Young poultry, on the other hand, is ideal for roasting and frying.

Before freezing your poultry, prepare it according to how you intend to use it in the future. Birds cut up for specific recipes must be chopped up before freezing. The same is true for cooked birds in half or whole. However, the stuffing inside stuffed poultry should not be frozen. The stuffing is more likely to contain toxic bacteria during thawing and refreezing. The filling can be frozen separately from the poultry. The giblets, gizzard, heart, liver, and neck should also be packed separately because they spoil faster, in about two weeks. These are excellent for making gravy or stuffing.

Pack chopped-up birds in the same manner as you would other red meats. Place freezer paper between individual portions to make separation easier when taking them out. You can also tray individual pack pieces of poultry, which, like red meats, come wrapped in butcher paper when purchased fresh from butcher shops and stores. These papers will not keep your birds from getting burned in the freezer. If you intend to keep these birds in your freezer for more than a week, rewrap or overwrap them until they arrive vacuum-sealed. If they are, do not open them; simply place them in the freezer.

Fish

Fish is much more challenging to prepare than red meat because it spoils quickly. If you catch them fresh, in addition to gutting, descaling, and cleaning them, you should also salt them or dunk them in an ascorbic acid solution to improve their shelf life. So, if you buy them from a fishmonger, ask them to gut, clean, and descale the fish. This will speed up your freezing preparation when you get home.

Freshly caught fish must be frozen immediately, so if you're out on the lake and don't plan on returning home soon, keep your fish packed deep within a large cooler filled with crushed ice. When you get home, thoroughly wash the fish in fresh potable water, then descale it by gently running the back of your knife back and forth against the skin. To remove the entrails, cut the fish's belly. When cutting, be careful not to puncture the innards, as this will impart a bitter taste to your fish. Remove the fish's head and rinse everything in fresh potable water again, paying particular attention to the fish's stomach cavity.

The back and dorsal fins are then removed with a sharp knife. Cut from the base, not leaving any fin stumps in the fish. To remove all the fins cleanly, cut along the side of the fish. Rinse the fish in water once more. After taking larger fish out of the freezer, it is recommended that they be chopped up or filleted for easier cooking. Larger fish, such as tuna or salmon, and large Spanish mackerels, should be cut into 34-inch-thick crosswise steaks.

Cut the back of a medium-sized fish, from the collarbone to the tail, to fillet it. Make another cut along the fish's tail, flattening the knife and slicing the flesh off, running the knife along the spine from the tail to the collarbone. Flip the fish over and repeat the procedure on the other side. Feel for fish bones stuck inside the flesh by running the back of your knife along the fish's spine. Pull out all of the fish bones with a tweezer.

To improve the quality of the fish, pre-treat it before freezing. This will reduce rancidity and the likelihood of flavor change. Dip fish with high-fat content, such as tuna, salmon, mackerel, trout, and mullet, in an ascorbic acid solution for 20 to 30 seconds.

To make the solution, combine two teaspoons of crystalline ascorbic acid and one quart of fresh potable water. Immerse lean fish like snapper, grouper, flounder, cod, croaker, redfish, whiting, and most freshwater species like bass, catfish, and crappie in brine for 20 to 30 seconds. The brine solution combines 14 cups of salt and 1 quart of fresh and cold potable water. This solution will firm the flesh and reduce drip loss when thawing the fish.

After pre-treatment, you have three options for freezing fish. The most convenient method is to wrap it in freezer wrap or place it in a freezer bag. Remove the air from the bag and place it directly in the freezer. For easier thawing, place freezer paper or baking paper between individual slices before freezing, just as you would with individual pieces of meat and poultry.

You can also put it in a rigid container and cover it with fresh potable water before freezing it. Cover the container tightly with an airtight lid or freezer-safe wrap after covering all parts of the fish with water.

You can also use the ice glaze method. This method is primarily used with vacuum-packed, frozen fish commonly found in supermarkets. To do this, unwrap and separate the fish (whole, cut, or filleted) in a tray and freeze. Once completely frozen, quickly immerse the fish or individual pieces of it in very cold, fresh potable water, then place it back in the freezer. Dunk and refreeze the fish several times until a uniform and visible layer of hard ice coats it. This will form a thin layer of water on the fish's surface, protecting it from the harsh environment of the freezer. Afterward, place the ice-glazed fish in a freezer bag and freeze it. Also, keep individual pieces separate from one another.

Fish roe, a delicacy in and of itself, should be frozen separately. Roe is the most perishable part of the fish and should be carefully removed from the stomach cavity and thoroughly washed with fresh potable water. To prepare the egg sacs for freezing, pierce them in several places with a clean and disinfected needle, then dunk them in an ascorbic acid solution like you would with fatty fish. A dip of 20 to 30 seconds would suffice. This will also reduce the rancidity and flavor change effect on the fish eggs when stored in the freezer. After that, freeze the egg sacs in individual freezer wraps or bags. Remember to use up the roe within three months.

Game

To prevent spoilage when storing fresh-caught wild game in the freezer, field dress and process large animals such as deer, antelope, and moose. As with other red meats, butcher and clean the meat before freezing it. Remove the bloodshot meat and discard it before freezing the meat. This will spoil faster and should be thrown away.

Squirrels and rabbits, for example, should be skinned, dressed, and refrigerated or chilled as soon as possible after being killed. Refrigerate it for a day or two until the meat is pliable and no longer rigid. Prepare or cut the meat as you intend to cook it in the future—pack and freeze as you would any other red meat.

Duck, geese, dove, quail, and pheasant should be bled, plucked of feathers, gutted, cleaned, and refrigerated or chilled immediately after shooting. Remember to trim or cut off any excess fat to prevent rancidity, especially on geese and ducks. Pack and freeze these game birds in the same manner as you would other poultry.

Thawing

To avoid the growth of bacteria that can cause spoilage, it is strongly advised to thaw meat, fish, and poultry in the refrigerator. Meats such as steaks and other large cuts of meat and whole poultry should be partially thawed before being placed in a pot or oven to cook. Larger pieces of meat and poultry can be partially thawed to avoid being overdone on the outside and undercooked or raw on the inside.

Frozen meats, fish, and poultry that will be breaded or battered before cooking, on the other hand, should be partially thawed so that the breading batter adheres to the surface. It is preferable to thaw frozen food before completely deep-frying it. Because of the high heat and short cooking time, the outside will be cooked quickly while the inside or center will remain frozen.

Cooking frozen meat takes a long time and should be done slowly over low heat. Cooking at high temperatures results in unbalanced cooking: the surface will char or cook quickly, but the inside will remain cold and frozen. If this is possible with chilled or refrigerated items, the likelihood of serving a charred but frozen inside roast with frozen meats is higher. Depending on the size of the cuts, frozen food will generally take half or twice the time that chilled or room temperature meat, fish, or poultry would.

There are three methods for thawing meats, poultry, and fish straight from the freezer. The quickest and safest method would be to thaw the sealed packages in the refrigerator. Place it on a tray or other container to catch drippings and keep meltwater from flooding your fridge. Smaller cuts will, of course, thaw much faster, taking only a few hours, but larger whole birds and larger cuts of meat may take a day or more to defrost thoroughly.

Submerging the sealed package in a bowl of room temperature water is an old method for thawing or defrosting frozen food. Replace the water every half hour until the item is completely defrosted. To avoid spoilage, the items must be cooked immediately after being thawed using this method.

When you buy microwaves, many of them come with a defrost function. As long as they fit inside the oven, these can also be used to defrost meats, fish, and poultry. You may need to turn and flip the items while defrosting to ensure that everything thaws evenly. Food defrosted in the microwave must be cooked immediately after defrosting, like food defrosted by submerging it in water.

Frozen meats, fish, and poultry should never be left to defrost at room temperature. This causes the bacteria to multiply rapidly, contaminating your food.

Before defrosted raw food items can be safely frozen again, they must be completely defrosted and cooked. Thawing or defrosting and then freezing again will result in larger ice crystals than desired. The meat's cell walls will rupture, causing the meat's quality to deteriorate over time. Cook them after defrosting to reduce moisture, flavor, and quality loss before freezing them again. However, it is perfectly safe to defrost an item inside the refrigerator and then change your mind and need to freeze it again. However, doing so will reduce the quality of the meat.

Flash Freezing

Individual food portions should be flash-frozen in a single layer on a parchment-lined tray to allow for easy separation. For easier storage, place the frozen items in heavy-duty resealable plastic bags. The following are the best flash freeze items:

- Avocado
- Banana
- Snap or shelled beans
- Berries
- Coconut
- Kernels of corn
- Flours
- Grains (raw and cooked)
- Seeds and nuts
- Shelled peas
- Stone fruits

The greater the surface area of an item, the greater its exposure to the elements and the shorter its storage time. A cut of meat, for example, will keep longer than ground beef. Similarly, preparing animal proteins before freezing reduces storage time compared to freezing them in their raw state. Foods with a high-fat content will also have a shorter storage life.

Beans and grains don't have their section here, but that doesn't mean they can't be frozen. On the contrary, they are excellent for freezing. The rules are the same regardless of the type of cooking.

Cooked grains can be flash-frozen by spreading them on a parchment-lined baking sheet and freezing them. Transfer to a labeled heavy-duty resealable plastic bag once frozen. Freeze beans in their cooking liquid in a pint or quart-size container or flat in a bag in the same manner. They will keep in the freezer for six months. Thaw in the refrigerator overnight, microwave, or reheat on the stovetop in a covered container over low heat.

Meat, Poultry, and Proteins

Thaw meats and proteins in the fridge for best quality—this could take overnight or several days, depending on the size of the pieces. Some frozen items, such as dinners and casseroles, can be cooked directly from the freezer. You can also place the meat in its wrapping in a bowl of cool water on the counter, changing the water frequently to keep it cool. Alternatively, you can thaw in the microwave at 50% power, but check it often so it doesn't start to cook.

Item	Months To Keep Frozen
Bacon and sausage	1 to 2
Casseroles	2 to 3
Egg whites or egg substitute	12
Frozen dinners and entrées	3 to 4
Gravy, meat, or poultry	2 to 3
Ham, hot dogs, lunch meats	1 to 2
Meat, cooked	2 to 3
Meat, uncooked ground	3 to 4
Meat, uncooked roasts	4 to 12
Meat, uncooked steaks, or chops	4 to 12

Poultry, cooked	4
Poultry, uncooked giblets	3 to 4
Poultry, uncooked parts	9
Poultry, uncooked whole	12
Soups and stews	2 to 3
Wild game, uncooked	8 to 12

Fruits

Many fruits can be flash-frozen and then kept frozen, but some foods benefit from pre-treatment. All of these fruits will keep in the freezer for nine months to a year in general but check them periodically to ensure they aren't developing freezer burn and that the packaging is still intact. You can use these straight from the freezer for baking or smoothies or heat them up for sauces and compotes. Fruit that has been frozen can also be a tasty and refreshing snack. Remember that their texture will be softer than fresh fruits, so choose a cooking method that considers this.

Type of Food	Prep Notes
Apples	Peel, core, slice, and dip into acidulated water; can sprinkle with sugar or turn into applesauce
Apricots	Pit; ascorbic acid dip; sugar sprinkle (optional); can puree
Bananas	Peel and slice; ascorbic acid dip; can mash
Blueberries	Blanch for 30 seconds for a firm texture; sugar sprinkle for a soft texture; can crush/puree
Cherries	Stem and pit; sugar sprinkle
Citrus	Peel, segment, or pull apart; sugar sprinkle (optional); can juice
Cranberries	Blanch for 30 seconds for a firm texture; sugar sprinkle for a soft texture; can crush/puree
Figs	Peel (optional); sugar sprinkle (optional); can crush
Grapes	Sugar sprinkle (optional); can juice

Guava	Peel and cut; sugar sprinkle (optional); can puree (add lemon juice)
Loquats	Cut and seed; acidulated water; can puree (add juice)
Mango	Peel and slice; sugar sprinkle (optional); can puree
Melons	Peel, remove soft areas, cube, slice, or ball; sugar sprinkle (optional); can crush (add lemon juice)
Peaches and nectarines	Peel, pit, and slice; acidulated water dip; sugar dip; can crush/puree
Pears	Peel, core, and slice; acidulated water dip; sugar sprinkle (optional); can puree
Persimmons	Peel and cut; can puree (add juice)
Pineapple	Peel, remove eyes/core; dice or slice; sugar sprinkle (optional); can crush
Plums	Cut and pit; acidulated water dip; sugar dip; can puree (use juice)
Rhubarb	Cut into 1-to 2-inch pieces; blanch for 1 minute; sugar sprinkle (optional); can puree (cook in boiling water)

Vegetables

Most vegetables must be pre-treated in some way before freezing. Vegetables can be stored in the freezer for nine months to a year, but check them regularly to ensure they don't develop freezer burn and that the packaging is still intact. For a quick side dish, stir into casseroles, roast straight from the freezer, or heat on the stovetop or microwave. Like fresh fruit, the texture of vegetables will be softer than when cooked, so use a cooking method that takes this into account.

Type of Food	Prep Notes
Asparagus	Trim and blanch
Beets	Roast or boil until thoroughly cooked; peel. If small, freeze whole, or quarter and flash freeze
Broccoli and cauliflower	Separate florets, chop stems, blanch

Broccoli rabe	Trim, chop, and blanch
Brussels sprouts	Halve large sprouts, keep small ones whole; blanch
Carrots	Slice or chop; blanch
Celery	Slice or chop
Corn	Blanch on the cob, then cut off kernels
Eggplant	Slice or halve (if small), salt for 30 minutes, then roast until tender
Fennel bulb	Core, slice, and roast until tender, or chop and freeze (the texture will suffer if you don't pre-cook, so this is appropriate for soups and casseroles)
Garlic	Roast whole, then puree or mash the cloves; freeze in ice-cube trays
Ginger	Grate or juice and freeze in ice-cube trays, or freeze, whole and unpeeled, in plastic wrap—to use, grate from frozen
Green beans	Trim and blanch
Hardy greens	Sauté, cool, and freeze in a heavy-duty resealable plastic bag
Herbs	Blend with water or oil and freeze in ice-cube trays
Leeks	Slice or chop
Mushrooms	Slice or chop, dip in acidulated water, then steam blanch, sauté, or roast
Okra	Trim and blanch
Onions and shallots	Slice or chop
Parsnips	Slice or chop, then blanch
Peppers, sweet and hot	Slice, chop, or leave whole if small; can roast before freezing
Potatoes	Peel, chop, blanch, or roast (do not need to cook fully)
Scallions	Puree or finely chop, mix with water or oil; freeze in ice-cube trays

Spinach and other tender greens	Sauté, cool, and freeze in a heavy-duty resealable plastic bag
Squash, summer	Slice 1/2 inch thick and blanch
Squash, winter	Roast and mash, or cube and blanch until fully cooked
Sweet potatoes	Peel, chop, blanch, or roast (do not need to cook fully)
Tomatillos	Remove husks, score, freeze whole or roast and freeze
Tomatoes	Blanch and peel, or freeze whole or chopped, or roast and freeze

Troubleshooting

Issue	Root Cause	Solution	Keep/Toss
The surface of food is light colored; food is tough or dried out	Freezer burn; food exposed to air	Seal food tightly, making sure there are no tears/rips Use vacuum-seal bags Remove as much air as possible from the bag	Keep, but taste and consistency will be altered
Brownish color in vegetables	No blanching	Blanch vegetables before freezing	Keep, but taste and consistency will be altered
Food is mushy	Freezer burn; food exposed to air Temperature fluctuation Food too large or dense when	Seal food tightly, making sure there are no tears/rips Use vacuum-seal bags Remove as much air as possible from the bag Freeze foods at 0°F or	Toss

	frozen	below and maintain the temperature during storage Freeze smaller portions	
Watery/gummy in consistency fruits	Freezer burn; food exposed to air Temperature fluctuation Food too large or dense when frozen	Seal food tightly, making sure there are no tears/rips Use vacuum-seal bags Remove as much air as possible from the bag Freeze foods at 0°F or below and maintain the temperature during storage Freeze smaller portions	Toss
Discoloration in fruits	No pre-treatment	Light-colored fruits need to be treated in sugar syrup or citric acid.	Safe, but the taste and appearance will be altered

How to Properly Store Frozen Food

Although frozen food can be stored for long periods, its quality and nutrition degrade over time. Even though food can be stored in the freezer indefinitely, don't try to keep it for 50,000 years. Eating beef sitting in the back of your freezer for over a decade is still dangerous. Here's a convenient list that shows how long food can be kept in the freezer.

Seafood

- 2 to 3 months for fatty fish (perch, salmon, and mackerel).
- 3 to 6 months for lean fish (flounder, cod, and sole).

- 4 to 6 months for cooked fish
- 2 months for smoked fish (sealed and vacuum-packed)
- 3 to 6 months for shellfish (e.g., mussels, oysters, scallops)
- 3 to 5 months for shrimp
- 2 months for cooked crab

Processed Meat

- 1 to 2 months for bacon
- 1 to 2 months for luncheon meat (open/sealed package or deli-sliced)
- 3 to 4 months for burgers and ground meat patties (beef, pork, poultry, veal, lamb, and other meats)
- 1 to 2 months for (opened or sealed) hot dogs
- 1 to 2 months for raw sausages (made from beef, chicken, pork, or turkey)
- 1 to 2 months for cooked sausages (made from beef, chicken, pork, or turkey)
- 2 months of pre-frozen sausages (made from beef, chicken, pork, or turkey)
- 5 to 6 months for fresh ham, uncooked and uncured
- 3 to 4 months for fresh ham, cooked and uncured
- 1 to 2 months for fresh ham cured, cooked, and vacuum sealed (unopened)
- 1 month for country ham
- Canned and unopened (labeled "keep refrigerated"): no need to freeze; it will last 6 to 9 months in the fridge
- 1 to 2 months if canned and opened (shelf-stable)
- 1 month for Italian and Spanish hams (Parma, Prosciutto, Serrano, and so on)
- 2 to 3 months for lamb and beef fresh ground meat
- 1 to 2 months for pork fresh ground meat
- 6 to 12 months for beef slices, fresh whole (for steaks and chops)

- 3 to 6 months for pork slices, fresh whole (for steaks and chops)
- 1 to 2 months for veal and lamb slices, fresh whole (for steaks and chops)
- 6 to 12 months for fresh beef (for roasts)
- 3 to 6 months for fresh pork (for roasts)
- 6 to 9 months for fresh lamb and veal (for roasts)

Poultry

- 12 months for a whole chicken
- 6 months for chopped or cut chicken
- 12 months for a whole turkey
- 6 months for chopped or cut turkey
- 6 months for an entire goose and duck
- 3 months for giblets
- 8 to 12 months for uncooked wild game

Pre-Cooked and Cooked Food

- 3 months for stews or casseroles (meat, poultry, and fish)
- 3 months for meat pies
- 8 months for fruit pies (unbaked)
- 2 to 4 months for baked fruit pies
- 3 months for bread
- 3 months for the cake
- 3 months for cookies (baked and unbaked)
- 6 to 9 months for dairy butter
- 12 months for margarine
- 1 month for fresh milk
- 2 months for heavy cream
- 1 month for whipped cream
- 2 months for ice cream
- 5 to 8 weeks for organic and natural cheeses
- 4 months for processed cheeses

Eggs

- 12 months for raw beaten eggs (raw eggs keep better in the freezer when beaten)
- 12 months for Raw eggs (in shells); however, keep refrigerated until thawed.

Overall, food appropriately stored in subzero temperatures will keep you going for a long time, if not indefinitely, but be careful if the frozen item has been sleeping in the back of a freezer for years. Avoid eating food that appears and smells off or rotten to avoid food poisoning.

Recipes

Teriyaki Marinade

Preparation time: 10 minutes | Cooking time: 35 minutes

Servings: 1 cup

Ingredients:

- 1/3 c. soy sauce
- 1/3 c. rice wine vinegar
- 3 tbsp. olive oil
- 2 tbsp. light brown sugar
- 1 tsp. thinly sliced garlic or 1/2 teaspoon garlic powder
- 1 tsp. grated peeled fresh ginger or 1/2 teaspoon ground ginger

Directions:

1. In a medium bowl, large measuring cup, or jar, combine the soy sauce, vinegar, oil, sugar, garlic, and ginger. Whisk well to combine.
2. If you are freezing the marinade alone, pour it into a plastic pint container, or freeze flat in a heavy-duty resealable plastic bag.
3. If you are freezing the marinade with chicken, tofu, or tempeh, place the protein in a vacuum or heavy-duty resealable plastic bag. Pour the marinade into the bag. Close the bag, removing as much air as possible.
4. Place the bag on a flat dish in the freezer for 3 hours or until frozen solid. Check the bag to ensure there are no leaks—label and use within three months.

Tomato Paste

Preparation time: 30 minutes, plus 1 hour to cool

Cooking time: 4 to 26 hours | Servings: 4 half-pints or 32 ice cubes

Ingredients:

- 12 lbs. tomatoes, cored and chopped (4 quarts); if you don't have a food mill, blanch and peel the tomatoes before coring and chopping
- 2 bay leaves
- 1/2 tsp. Diamond Crystal kosher salt (optional)

Directions:

1. If using a food mill, skip this step. In a large pot over high heat, cook the chopped tomatoes for 30 minutes, stirring frequently and crushing them with a wooden spoon to break them down and make them soft. Press the cooked tomatoes through a fine-mesh sieve into a slow cooker.
2. If using a food mill, pass the raw tomatoes through a food mill into a slow cooker.
3. Add the bay leaves to the cooker, cover the cooker, and cook on high heat for 2 hours. After 2 hours, the puree should be bubbling.
4. Turn the lid slightly to the side so there is an opening for air to escape, or use two wooden spoons to prop up the lid. The objective is to have air flowing out of the cooker while keeping the puree hot so it can reduce. Cook for 24 hours, checking it and stirring every so often. The paste is ready when it holds its shape on a spoon.
5. Alternatively, place the puree in a saucepan, add the bay leaves, and place the pan over medium heat. Cook for 1½ to 2 hours, frequently stirring to avoid burning. When the paste is thick and coats the spoon, remove it from the heat and let it cool for 1 hour.
6. Taste the paste; add the salt if using.

7. Once cooled, remove the bay leaves from the paste, spoon the paste into an ice-cube tray, and freeze for 1 hour.

8. Transfer the cubes into a heavy-duty resealable plastic bag when the paste is frozen. Keep frozen, labeled, for up to 6 months. If you have vacuum-sealed bags, portion the cubes into groups of 4 and vacuum seal the bags for freezing.

Chicken Bone Broth

Preparation time: 15 minutes | Cooking time: 8 hours 30 minutes (stovetop); 15 hours 30 minutes (slow cooker) | Makes: 4 quarts

Ingredients:

- 20 c. water
- Bones from 1 whole roasted chicken, picked clean of meat
- 1 yellow onion, quartered
- 1 celery stalk halved
- 3 carrots, roughly chopped
- 3 garlic cloves, peeled
- 1 bay leaf
- 2 tsp. Diamond Crystal kosher salt (optional), divided, plus more as needed

Directions:

1. In a slow cooker, combine the water, bones, onion, celery, carrots, garlic, bay leaf, and one teaspoon of salt (if using). Cover the cooker and cook on high heat for 10 to 15 minutes until the liquid starts to boil. If 20 cups of water are too much for your slow cooker, just cover the bones with water.

2. Once the broth boils, turn the slow cooker temperature to low. If you are making this on the stovetop, combine the ingredients in a large stockpot over high heat and bring it to a boil. Reduce the heat to low, partially cover the pot with a lid,

and simmer for 6 to 8 hours. With either appliance, maintain a simmer or low boil.

3. Check the broth at the 5-hour mark. You should start to see the chicken fat on the top of the broth and the vegetables softening.

4. After the 10-hour mark, the broth will start to become ready. The chicken bones should be brittle, and you can crush them easily.

5. By hour 15, the vegetables will almost disintegrate upon touching them. Taste the broth and turn off the heat.

6. Using a fine-mesh strainer set over a large heatproof bowl, filter out all the bones and vegetables from the broth. Taste the broth. Add the remaining teaspoon of salt (if used), stir, and taste again. If you need more salt, add it to taste.

7. Pour the broth into four quart-size plastic containers, leaving 1½ inches of headspace to allow the broth to expand while freezing—freeze, labeled, for up to 6 months.

Spinach and Parmesan Frittatas

Preparation time: 15 minutes| Cooking time: 35 minutes

Servings: 12 frittatas

Ingredients:

- 2 tbsp. olive oil or butter, divided
- 1 c. chopped onion
- 1 (16-ounce) package frozen spinach, thawed, squeezed dry, and chopped
- 12 large eggs
- 1/2 tsp. Diamond Crystal kosher salt
- 1/2 tsp. freshly ground black pepper
- 3/4 c. grated parmesan cheese

- 1 tbsp. dried parsley or dill (optional)

Directions:

1. Preheat the oven to 350°F. Coat a 12-cup muffin tin, or two 6-cup tins, using one tablespoon of oil.
2. Heat the remaining one tablespoon of oil over medium heat in a small skillet. Add the onion and cook for about 8 minutes, stirring, until soft.
3. Add the spinach and cook for 2 minutes, just until hot. Evenly distribute the vegetable mixture among the prepared cups.
4. Whisk the eggs, salt, and pepper in a large bowl until blended. Whisk in the cheese and dried herbs, if desired.
5. Pour the egg mixture into a large measuring cup and evenly distribute it into the muffin tin, using all the custard.
6. Bake for 25 minutes until the eggs are lightly browned on the top and sizzling on the sides.
7. Let cool to room temperature. Remove the cooled frittatas from the tin and place them into a heavy-duty resealable plastic bag—freeze, labeled, for up to 3 months.
8. To reheat, microwave on high power for 2 minutes.

Vegan Soup

Preparation time: 20 minutes | Cooking time: 30 minutes

Servings: 1 cup

Ingredients:

- 4 tbsp. of olive oil
- 2 c. chopped leeks, white part only (from approximately three medium leeks)
- 2 tbsp. finely minced garlic, Kosher salt
- 2 c. carrots, peeled and chopped into rounds (about two

medium)

- 2 c. peeled and diced potatoes
- 2 c. fresh green beans, broken or cut into 3/4-inch pieces
- 2 qt. of chicken or vegetable broth
- 4 c. peeled, seeded, and chopped tomatoes
- 2 ears of corn, kernels removed
- 1/2 tsp. freshly ground black pepper
- 1/4 c. packed, chopped fresh parsley leaves
- 1 to 2 tsp. freshly squeezed lemon juice

Directions:

1. In a sizable, heavy-bottomed stockpot, warm the olive oil over medium-low heat.
2. Once hot, add the leeks, garlic, and a dash of salt, and cook for 7 to 8 minutes, or until they start to soften.
3. Stirring occasionally, add the carrots, potatoes, and green beans. Cook for 4 to 5 minutes.
4. Add the stock, increase the heat to high, and bring to a simmer. Once simmering, add the tomatoes, corn kernels, and pepper.
5. Reduce the heat to low, cover, and cook until the vegetables are fork-tender, approximately 25 to 30 minutes.
6. Remove from heat and add the parsley and lemon juice – season to taste with kosher salt.
7. Serve immediately.

Pea, Scallion, and Ginger Ramen Soup

Preparation time: 15 minutes | Cooking time: 12 minutes

Servings: 2 cups

Ingredients:

- 1 tbsp bouillon granules
- 1 tbsp powdered soy sauce

- 1/2 tsp ground ginger
- 1/8 tsp ground garlic
- 1/8 teaspoon freshly ground black pepper
- 1/4 cup freeze-dried peas
- 2 tbsp freeze-dried scallions
- 1/2 cup Ramen noodles (broken)
- 1 3/4 cups boiling water (divided)

Directions:

1. Mix the bouillon powder, ground soy sauce, powdered garlic, fresh ginger, freeze-dried scallions and ramen noodles together in a Ziplock bag or jar that holds 1 quart. Mix well.
2. Mix the ingredients in a bowl or mug with a 2+ cup capacity.
3. Stir in half the boiling water and mix well until it is all incorporated. Stir in the remaining boiling water.
4. Cover with a towel and let it rest for between 8-10 minutes.
5. To freeze-dry the soup. First, spoon it onto the tray, and then spread it out to a thickness of approximately half an inch. Following the half-inch guideline when filling the tray is a solid starting point. Overfilling the tray will cause condensation within the freeze drier. After the food has been placed on the tray, now, place the tray into the freeze dryer's rack.
6. Put in the insulating pad, and close and secure the door. Push start. Freeze dryers include a built-in reminder to make sure the drain valve is shut. Push Continue, and it will start.
7. After it's done, extract the soup from the freeze dryer.
8. Place it in a Mylar bag with an oxygen-absorbing packet, seal it, and label it with the date.

NOTE: I have used Freeze Dryer to freeze-dry all the recipes. But for your convenience, you can use any of the methods mentioned in chapter 2.

Potato and Chive Freeze Dried Soup

Preparation time: 5 minutes | Cooking time: 15 minutes

Servings: 2 cups

Ingredients:

- 1/3 cup instant potato flakes
- 2 tbsp grated Parmesan cheese canned and dried
- 1 1/2 tsp cornstarch
- 1 tbsp freeze-dried chives
- 2 tbsp bouillon granules
- 1/4 cup powdered milk
- 1/8 tsp onion powder
- 1/8 Tsp garlic powder
- 1/8 teaspoon freshly ground black pepper
- 1/8 tsp salt
- 1 3/4 cups boiling water (divided)

Directions:

1. Add the instant potato chips, frozen cheese, cornstarch and freeze dried herbs, bouillon powder granules milk powder, powdered milk powder, onion powder, garlic powder, fresh ground black pepper salt, and powdered milk to a zip lock bag or jar with a 1 quart capacity. Mix well.
2. Mix the ingredients in a 2+ cup mug or bowl.
3. Stir in half the boiling water and mix well until it is all incorporated. Stir in the remaining boiling water.
4. Cover with a towel and let it rest for between 8-10 minutes.
5. To freeze-dry the soup. First, spoon it onto the tray, and then spread it out to a thickness of approximately half an inch. Place the tray into the freeze dryer's rack.
6. Put in the insulating pad, and close and secure the door. Push start.
7. After it's done, extract the soup from the freeze dryer.

8. Put it in a Mylar bag with an oxygen-absorbing packet, seal it, and label it with the date.

☆ ☆ ☆ ☆ ☆

Stuffed Pepper Soup

Preparation time: 5 minutes | Cooking time: 15 minutes

Servings: 2

Ingredients:

- 1/4 cup instant 1-minute rice
- 1/4 cup frozen-dried green bell peppers
- 1/4 cup frozen-dried red bell peppers
- 1/4 cup frozen-dried orange bell pepper
- 1/4 cup frozen-dried ground beef
- 1/4 cup frozen-dried tomato powder
- 3 cups boiling water (divided)
- To serve, pinch of oregano
- Serve with a pinch of thyme
- Splash of pepper sauce (to serve)

Directions:

1. To a zip lock bag, or jar, add the instant rice, freeze green bell peppers and red bell peppers as well as freeze dried orange bell peppers, frozen-dried ground beef and freeze dried tomato paste. Mix well.
2. Mix the ingredients in a 3+ cup mug or bowl.
3. Stir in half the water. Continue stirring until it is completely dissolved. Add the remaining boiling water to the bowl and stir.
4. Cover with a towel and let it rest for between 8-10 minutes.
5. Season the soup by adding a pinch of oregano, thyme, and a splash pepper sauce.

6. To freeze-dry the soup. First, spoon it onto the tray, and then spread it out to a thickness of approximately half an inch. Place the tray into the freeze dryer's rack.

7. Put in the insulating pad, and close and secure the door. Push start.

8. After it's done, extract the soup from the freeze dryer. Put it in a Mylar bag with an oxygenabsorbing packet, seal it, and label it with the date.

Thai Coconut Milk Soup with Rice

Preparation time: 5 minutes | Cooking time: 10 minutes

Servings: 2

Ingredients:

- 1/2 cup powdered coconut milk
- 1 1/2 tbsp bouillon granules)
- 1 tsp powdered soy sauce
- 1/2 tsp brown sugar
- 2 tsp cornstarch
- 1/2 tsp dried basil
- 1/2 tsp ground ginger
- 1/8 tsp ground garlic
- Ground cayenne in a pinch
- 1/5 tsp powdered lime juice crystals powder
- 1/4 cup chopped freeze-dried mushrooms
- 1 tbsp freeze-dried scallions
- 2 tbsp freeze-dried peas
- 1/4 cup instant 1-minute Rice
- 1 3/4 cups boiling water (divided)

Directions:

1. You can add the powdered coconut milk and bouillon powder

granules, as well as brown sugar, cornstarch or dried ginger, ground garlic, cayenne pepper, lime juice crystals and freeze-dried mushrooms, freeze -dried scallions and freeze-dried peas to a jar, or Ziplock bag that holds a 1-quart jar. Mix the ingredients together by stirring or massaging them until they are well combined.

2. Mix the ingredients in a 2+ cup mug or bowl.
3. Stir in half the boiling water and mix well until it is all incorporated. Stir in the remaining boiling water.
4. Cover with a towel and let it rest for between 8-10 minutes.
5. To freeze-dry the soup and rice. First, spoon them onto the trays, and then spread it out to a thickness of approximately half an inch. Place the trays into the freeze dryer's rack.
6. Put in the insulating pad, and close and secure the door. Push start.
7. After it's done, extract the trays from the freeze dryer. Put it in a Mylar bag with an oxygenabsorbing packet, seal it, and label it with the date.

Chicken Noodle Skillet Meal in a Jar

Preparation time: 5 minutes | Cooking time: 10 minutes

Servings: 2

Ingredients:

- 2 cups egg noodles
- 1 tbsp minced, dehydrated onions
- 1/3 cup instant non-fat dried milk
- 1 1/2 teaspoons Italian seasoning
- 1/2 tsp salt
- 1/4 tsp pepper
- 1/4 cup butter powder

- 1/2 cup freeze-dried vegetable mix
- 1/3 cup cheese powder
- 1 cup frozen-dried diced chicken
- 3 1/2 cups water

Directions:

1. In a large-mouthed Mason Jar, layer the ingredients according to recipe order: egg noodles, minced onion, non-fat dry milk, Italian seasoning, salt and pepper, butter powder. To settle, shake gently.

2. Place a canning lid over the jar. Seal it with a vacuum seal. Add a ring and tighten by hand, taking care to not overtighten.

3. You can label the jar with the date and keep it dry in a cool, dry place.

4. Once you're ready to cook, transfer the contents of the jar to a skillet.

5. Bring to boil the water. Reduce the heat and simmer for between 12-15 minutes, stirring occasionally.

6. Remove the pan from the heat. Allow the sauce to cool for about 3-5 minutes. Enjoy and serve.

7. To freeze-dry the meal. First, spoon it onto the tray, and then spread it out to a thickness of approximately half an inch. Place the tray into the freeze dryer's rack.

8. Put in the insulating pad, and close and secure the door. Push start.

9. After it's done, extract the tray from the freeze dryer. Put it in a Mylar bag with an oxygenabsorbing packet, seal it, and label it with the date.

Egg Fried Rice

Preparation time: 5 minutes | Cooking time: 15 minutes

Servings: 2

Ingredients:

- 1 cup freeze-dried mixed veggies
- 1 vegetable bouillon cube
- 1/2 tsp ground ginger
- 1/2 tsp brown sugar
- 1/4 tsp garlic powder
- 2 Single-portion sachets with soy sauce
- Instant rice in 60 seconds
- 1/4 cup whole eggs crystals
- Water (as required)

Directions:

1. Prepare three Ziplock bags while you are at home.
2. Combine the mixed vegetables with the bouillon cubes, ground ginger, sugar and garlic powder in the first bag.
3. You can add the rice to another bag, and the egg crystals in the third.
4. Combine the egg crystals and 3 ounces of water in a saucepan. Stir well to combine.
5. Place the pot on the stovetop and, using low heat, cook the eggs crystals, stirring constantly. Once the egg is cooked, take it out of the pot and place it on a plate.
6. To the pot, add 1 1/4 cups water and the contents from the first Ziplock bag. Reduce the heat to low and let the vegetables simmer for 5 minutes.
7. Stir in the rice. Remove the pot from the heat. Cover the pot with a lid. Let the pot cool for five minutes.
8. Mix the egg back into the pot. Stir the eggs well to combine and heat the eggs.

9. To freeze-dry the rice. First, spoon them onto the trays, and then spread it out to a thickness of approximately half an inch. Place the trays into the freeze dryer's rack.

10. Put in the insulating pad, and close and secure the door. Push start.

11. After it's done, extract the trays from the freeze dryer. Put it in a Mylar bag with an oxygenabsorbing packet, seal it, and label it with the date.

Jambalaya with Orzo

Preparation time: 5 minutes | Cooking time: 12 minutes

Servings: 6

Ingredients:

- 1 cup orzo pasta
- 1/2 cup freeze-dried vegetables
- 2 tbsp tomato powder
- 1 tbsp Cajun seasoning
- 1 tsp salt
- 1 tbsp olive oil
- 3 ounces spicy smoked sausage
- 2 1/2 cups water

Directions:

1. When you get home, put the orzo pasta and freeze-dried vegetables, tomato powder, Cajun seasoning and salt in a Ziplock container. Separately pack the oil and spicy-smoked sausage.

2. Add the contents of the Ziplock bag outside your home to a pan.

3. Add the water to the pan. Then, heat the oil in the pan and

continue cooking for about 8-10 minutes until the orzo becomes al dente.

4. While the sausage is heating, cut it and place it in a pan.

5. To freeze-dry the meal. First, spoon it onto the trays, and then spread it out to a thickness of approximately half an inch. Place the trays into the freeze dryer's rack.

6. Put in the insulating pad, and close and secure the door. Push start.

7. After it's done, extract the trays from the freeze dryer. Put it in a Mylar bag with an oxygenabsorbing packet, seal it, and label it with the date.

Pasta Carbonara

Preparation time: 5 minutes | Cooking time: 7 minutes

Servings: 2

Ingredients:

- 4 ounces uncooked angel hair pasta
- 1/2 tsp salt
- 1 tbsp olive oil
- 2 tbsp whole eggs crystals
- 2 tbsp grated, dried and canned Parmesan cheese
- 1/2 tsp black pepper
- 2 ounces bacon jerky

Directions:

1. At home, place the angel hair pasta, salt, and oil in a large Ziplock bag. In a separate container, add the oil.

2. In a second Ziplock bag, add the egg crystals and grated Parmesan cheese. As needed, repackage the bacon jelly.

3. Add the pasta and salt outside your home to the crockpot. Add

enough water to cover the pasta and then add the olive oil. Bring to a boil, and cook the pasta until it is al dente.

4. Reduce the heat to low and add the egg crystals, Parmesan cheese and stir well. If too much of the mixture has boiled, you may need to add some water.

5. Turn off the heat source and add the bacon jerky. Serve and enjoy.

6. To freeze-dry the pasta. First, spoon it onto the trays, and then spread it out to a thickness of approximately half an inch. Place the trays into the freeze dryer's rack.

7. Put in the insulating pad, and close and secure the door. Push start.

8. After it's done, extract the trays from the freeze dryer. Put it in a Mylar bag with an oxygenabsorbing packet, seal it, and label it with the date.

Thai Red Curry Rice with Coconut Milk Sauce

Preparation time: 5 minutes | Cooking time: 8 minutes

Servings: 3

Ingredients:

- 1/2 cup instant 60-second rice
- 1/4 cup frozen-dried mixed vegetables
- 1/4 cup freeze-dried chicken
- 3 tbsp coconut milk powder
- 2 tbsp Thai Red Curry Powder
- 1 tbsp peanut butter powder
- 1 tbsp peanuts (chopped)
- 1/2 sachet crystallized lime

- 1/2 tsp salt
- 3/4 cup water
- 1 tbsp oil

Directions:

1. At home, combine the dry ingredients in a Ziplock bag (rice, freeze-dried mixed veggies, freeze-dried chicken, powdered milk, curry powder, powdered peanut butter, peanuts, lime, and salt). Shake to combine. Double bag for transport to prevent the curry from infiltrating your purse or backpack.
2. Outside your home, bring the water to a boil.
3. Add the Ziplock bag's contents to the pot along with the oil and stir to combine.
4. Cover with a lid and simmer for 4-6 minutes, until the rice, chicken, and veggies are rehydrated.
5. To freeze-dry the meal. First, spoon it onto the trays, and then spread it out to a thickness of approximately half an inch. Place the trays into the freeze dryer's rack.
6. Put in the insulating pad, and close and secure the door. Push start.
7. After it's done, extract the trays from the freeze dryer. Put it in a Mylar bag with an oxygenabsorbing packet, seal it, and label it with the date.

Apple Crisp

Preparation time: 5 minutes | Cooking time: 8 minutes

Servings: 2

Ingredients:

- 1 1/2 cups freeze-dried apples
- 3 tbsp brown sugar
- 1 tsp ground cinnamon

- 1/4 tsp ground cloves
- 1/3 cup granola
- 1/4 cup walnuts (chopped)

Directions:

1. While at home, add the apples, followed by the sugar, ground cinnamon, and ground cloves, to a Ziplock bag.
2. Using a second smaller Ziplock bag, combine the granola with the chopped walnuts.
3. Outside your home, transfer the apple mixture to a cookpot.
4. Add approximately 3 cups of water to the mixture, and stir to combine. Light a stove, and cook over moderate to low heat until the apples start to soften and the sugar is dissolved. You will need to stir the mixture to thicken and add a drop of more water if necessary.
5. When the apple mixture is ready, take the pot off the heat.
6. Scatter the granola and walnuts over the granola and enjoy.
7. To freeze-dry the apple crisps. First, spoon it onto the trays, and then spread it out to a thickness of approximately half an inch. Place the trays into the freeze dryer rack.
8. Put in the insulating pad, and close and secure the door. Push start.
9. After it's done, extract the tray from the freeze dryer. Put it in a Mylar bag with an oxygen absorbing packet, seal it, and label it with the date.

Feta Cheese Topped Moussaka

Preparation time: 5 minutes | Cooking time: 2 hours

Servings: 2

Ingredients:

- 4 large aubergines (thinly sliced diagonally)

- Olive oil
- 2 pound 2 ounces minced lamb
- 2 large-size onions (peeled, chopped)
- 4 cloves garlic (peeled, crushed)
- 4 tbsp tomato puree
- 1 tsp ground cinnamon
- 1 1/2 tbsp dried mixed herbs
- 2 (14 1/2 ounce) cans chopped tomatoes

Topping:

- 2 large-size eggs
- 17 1/2 ounces plain Greek yogurt
- 7 ounces Greek feta cheese (crumbled)
- Black pepper
- 2 tbsp Parmesan cheese (finely grated)

Directions:

1. Preheat the main oven to 425 degrees F.
2. Brush one side of the sliced aubergines with a drop of oil and arrange on 2 large baking sheets.
3. In batches, if necessary, roast the aubergine in the preheated oven for 20 minutes, flipping over halfway and brushing with a drop more oil. Roast until fork tender and golden. Set to one side in a bowl and repeat with the remaining aubergine.
4. Reduce the oven temperature to 395 degrees F.
5. In the meantime, heat a large casserole dish over high heat. When sufficiently hot add the lamb mince and cook while breaking the meat up using the back of a spoon for 5 minutes.
6. Stir in the onions along with the garlic and cook until the lamb is browned and the onions, softened; this will take around 5 minutes.
7. Transfer the lamb mixture to a colander to drain away any fat, return to the dish.
8. Next, add the tomato puree, cinnamon, and mixed herbs, cook

for 60 seconds.

9. Stir in the canned tomatoes, to combine. Add sufficient cold water to one empty can to fill it halfway full and tip the contents into the dish.

10. Season and rapidly simmer, while occasionally stirring for 15 minutes, until the majority of the liquid has evaporated.

11. In the meantime, prepare the topping. In a bowl, combine the eggs with the Greek yogurt. Stir in the feta cheese and season liberally with pepper.

12. Layer the moussaka. Evenly divide half of the lamb mince between two, deep 2-quart oven and freezer safe dishes.

13. Evenly divided the roasted aubergines between the two dishes and arrange on top of the mince. Season and repeat the layers, finishing with aubergine.

14. Divide the topping between them, evenly spread to cover the aubergine layer. Scatter Parmesan over the top.

15. Set one moussaka aside to completely cool, for freezing.

16. Place the second moussaka on a baking tray and cook in the preheated oven for between 3540 minutes, until the cheese is golden and the meat is piping hot. You may need to cover the moussaka in foil to avoid it browning too quickly.

17. Serve and enjoy.

18. To freeze-dry the meal. First, spoon it onto the tray, and then spread it out to a thickness of approximately half an inch. Place the tray into the freeze dryer's rack.

19. Put in the insulating pad, and close and secure the door. Push start.

20. After it's done, extract the tray from the freeze dryer. Put it in a Mylar bag with an oxygenabsorbing packet, seal it, and label it with the date.

Tomato Soup with Whole Wheat Orzo

Preparation time: 5 minutes | Cooking time: 30 minutes

Servings: 4

Ingredients:

- 2 tbsp olive oil
- 1 medium-size onion (peeled and chopped)
- 1 1/4 cups uncooked whole wheat orzo pasta
- 2 (14 ounces) cans chopped whole tomatoes with juice
- 3 cups low-salt chicken broth
- 2 tsp dried oregano
- 1/4 tsp salt
- 1/4 tsp freshly ground black pepper
- Greek feta cheese (crumbled)
- Fresh basil (chopped, to serve)
- Crusty bread (to serve)

Directions:

1. In a large pan, over moderate heat, heat the oil.
2. Add the onion to the pan and sauté for 3-5 minutes, until tender.
3. Add the whole wheat orzo and cook while stirring until lightly toasted.
4. Stir in the drained tomatoes, chicken broth, dried oregano, salt, and black pepper. Bring to boil.
5. Turn the heat down and simmer, while covered for 15-20 minutes, or until the orzo is bitetender. Do this while occasionally stirring.
6. Garnish with crumbled feta and chopped basil – serve.
7. To freeze-dry the soup. First, spoon it onto the trays, and then spread it out to a thickness of approximately half an inch. Place the trays into the freeze dryer's rack.
8. Put in the insulating pad, and close and secure the door. Push

start.

9. After it's done, extract the trays from the freeze dryer. Put it in a Mylar bag with an oxygenabsorbing packet, seal it, and label it with the date.

Strawberry Lemonade Deep Dish Pie

Preparation time: 5 minutes | Cooking time: 10 minutes

Servings: 2

Ingredients:

- 2 1/2 cups frozen strawberry slices (thawed)
- 1 (3.4 ounce) container instant lemon pudding mix
- 8 ounces whipped topping
- 1 (9") graham cracker crust

Directions:

1. Combine the strawberries (along with any thawing juices) and the pudding mix. Set aside for 5 minutes. Fold in the whipped topping.
2. Spoon the mixture into the graham cracker crust.
3. To freeze-dry the dish. First, spoon it onto the tray, and then spread it out to a thickness of approximately half an inch. Place the tray into the freeze dryer's rack.
4. Put in the insulating pad, and close and secure the door. Push start.
5. After it's done, extract the tray from the freeze dryer. Put it in a Mylar bag with an oxygenabsorbing packet, seal it, and label it with the date.

Apple Crisp

Preparation time: 5 minutes | Cooking time: 50 minutes

Servings: 2

Ingredients:

Apples:

- 5 cups apples (cored, sliced)
- 1/4 cup brown sugar
- 1/2 tbsp fresh lemon juice
- Pinch nutmeg
- 1/2 tsp cinnamon
- 2 tbsp flour

Crisp:

- 4 cups brown sugar
- 4 cups flour
- 2 cups oats
- 1/2 tsp nutmeg
- 1 tsp cinnamon
- 2 cups salted butter (cubed)

Directions:

1. First, prepare the apples. Toss the apples together with the brown sugar, lemon juice, nutmeg, cinnamon, and flour in a large bowl. Divide the mixture between 6 small disposable, freezersafe aluminum trays.

2. Next, using clean hands, combine the sugar, flour, oats, nutmeg, and cinnamon together in a bowl. Rub in the cubes of butter until you form a crumbly mixture. Scatter the mixture evenly over the apples.

3. To freeze-dry the food. First, spoon it onto the tray, and then spread it out to a thickness of approximately half an inch. Place the tray into the freeze dryer rack.

4. Put in the insulating pad, and close and secure the door. Push start.

5. After it's done, extract the tray from the freeze dryer. Put it in a Mylar bag with an oxygenabsorbing packet, seal it, and label it with the date.

Lemon Meringue Freeze

Preparation time: 5 minutes | Cooking time: 5 hours

Servings: 3

Ingredients:

- 1 (4 1/2 ounce) package instant lemon pie filling
- 1 tbsp fresh lemon zest
- 3 ounces whipped topping
- 14 soft ladyfingers
- 1/2 cup fresh raspberries
- 1 tbsp lemon peel twists

Directions:

1. Prepare the pie filling as per the package directions and pour into a bowl.

2. Stir in the lemon zest and allow it to completely cool.

3. Prepare the whipped dessert topping mix as directed on the package directions and stir gently into the pie filling.

4. Cut a 2" piece from one end of each of the 14 ladyfingers and put to one side.

5. Arrange the ladyfingers, rounded-side out, around the rim of a 9" springform pan. They need to be standing up around the edge.

6. Use the trimmed pieces to cover the bottom of the pan.

7. Spoon the pie filling into the pan and freeze until firm, for

approximately 4 hours.

8. Heat the main oven to 425 degrees F.

9. Remove the rim of the springform pan.

10. Next, prepare the meringue as directed on the pie filling package and spread evenly over the dessert.

11. Bake until golden, for 5 minutes.

12. Top with fresh raspberries and lemon peel twists.

13. To freeze-dry the meal. First, spoon it onto the tray, and then spread it out to a thickness of approximately half an inch. Place the tray into the freeze dryer's rack.

14. Put in the insulating pad, and close and secure the door. Push start.

15. After it's done, extract the tray from the freeze dryer. Put it in a Mylar bag with an oxygen-absorbing packet, seal it, and label it with the date.

Maple Muffins

Preparation time: 5 minutes | Cooking time: 30 minutes

Servings: 2

Ingredients:

- 2 cups all-purpose flour
- 2 tsp baking powder
- 1/2 cup brown sugar
- 1/2 tsp salt
- 3/4 cup whole milk
- 1/2 cup salted butter (melted)
- 1/2 cup pure maple syrup
- 1/4 cup sour cream
- 1 large egg
- 1/2 tsp vanilla essence

Topping:

- 3 tbsp all-purpose flour
- 3 tbsp sugar
- 2 tbsp nuts (chopped)
- 1/2 tsp ground cinnamon
- 2 tbsp cold butter

Directions:

1. Preheat the main oven to 400 degrees F.
2. In a large mixing bowl, combine the flour with the baking powder, brown sugar, and salt.
3. In a second bowl, combine the milk with the butter, maple syrup, sour cream, egg, and vanilla essence. Add to the dry ingredients, and stir until just moistened.
4. Fill paper-lined muffin cups ⅔ full.
5. For the topping, combine the flour with the sugar, chopped nuts and cinnamon; cut in the butter until a crumbly consistency and sprinkle over batter.
6. Bake in the preheated oven for between 15-20 minutes.
7. Set aside to cool for 5 minutes before removing from the muffin cups to a wire baking rack.
8. Serve the muffins warm.
9. To freeze-dry the maple muffins. First, spoon them onto the trays, and then spread it out to a thickness of approximately half an inch. Place the trays into the freeze dryer's rack.
10. Put in the insulating pad, and close and secure the door. Push start.
11. After it's done, extract the trays from the freeze dryer. Put it in a Mylar bag with an oxygen-absorbing packet, seal it, and label it with the date.

Mini Watermelon and Lime Tarts

Preparation time: 5 minutes | Cooking time: 2 hours

Servings: 6

Ingredients:

- 2 cups seedless watermelon (cubed)
- 2 tbsp honey
- 1 cup Greek yogurt
- 1 tbsp fresh lime juice
- 1 1/2 tsp lime zest (grated)
- 2 tbsp slivered almonds (toasted)

Directions:

1. Add the watermelon to a food processor and blitz to a smooth puree. Divide the mixture between 8 cupcake liners. Freeze for an hour.

2. Combine the honey, yogurt, lime juice, and zest in a bowl. Spoon the mixture on top of the watermelon and sprinkle with toasted almonds. Return to the freezer for at least another hour.

3. To freeze-dry the dish. First, spoon it onto the tray, and then spread it out to a thickness of approximately half an inch. Place the tray into the freeze dryer's rack.

4. Put in the insulating pad, and close and secure the door. Push start.

5. After it's done, extract the tray from the freeze dryer. Put it in a Mylar bag with an oxygen-absorbing packet, seal it, and label it with the date.

Peanut Butter Choc Chip Banana Bread

Preparation time: 5 minutes | Cooking time: 1hour

Servings: 2

Ingredients:

- Nonstick spray
- 1 cup granulated sugar
- 2 cups all-purpose flour
- 1 tsp bicarb of soda
- 1 tsp baking powder
- 1 tsp pumpkin pie spice
- 1 tsp salt
- 2 large eggs (at room temperature)
- 4 ripe bananas (peeled, mashed)
- 1/4 cup unsweetened applesauce
- 1/2 cup smooth peanut butter
- 2 tsp vanilla essence
- 1/4 cup canola oil
- 2/3 cup semisweet choc chips

Directions:

1. Preheat the main oven to 350 degrees F.
2. Spritz three 4x3x2" loaf tins with nonstick spray.
3. Combine the sugar, flour, bicarb of soda, baking powder, pie spice, and salt in a bowl.
4. In a second bowl, beat together the eggs, banana, applesauce, peanut butter, vanilla essence, and canola oil.
5. Fold the dry mixture into the wet until incorporated.
6. Fold in the choc chips.
7. Divide the batter between the three loaf tins. Bake in the oven for just over 45 minutes until golden. Allow to cool completely.
8. To freeze-dry this recipe. First, put it onto the tray, and then

spread it out to a thickness of approximately half an inch. Place the trays into the freeze dryer's rack.

9. Put in the insulating pad, and close and secure the door. Push start.

10. After it's done, extract the tray from the freeze dryer. Put it in a Mylar bag with an oxygen-absorbing packet, seal it, and label it with the date.\

Garlic Lime Chicken

Preparation time: 5 minutes | Cooking time: 4 hours

Servings: 4

Ingredients:

- 2 1/2 pounds chicken breasts (trimmed, halved)
- 1/2 cup low sodium soy sauce
- 1/4 cup freshly squeezed lime juice
- 1 tbsp Worcestershire sauce
- 2 tbsp garlic (peeled, minced)
- 1/2 dry mustard
- 1/2 tsp ground black pepper
- 1/4 cup water

Directions:

1. Add the chicken breasts, soy sauce, lime juice, Worcestershire sauce, garlic, mustard, black pepper and water to a large Ziplock bag, seal, and gently shake to combine.

2. To freeze-dry the meal. First, spoon it onto the tray, and then spread it out to a thickness of approximately half an inch. Place the tray into the freeze dryer's rack.

3. Put in the insulating pad, and close and secure the door. Push start.

4. After it's done, extract the tray from the freeze dryer. Put it in

a Mylar bag with an oxygen-absorbing packet, seal it, and label it with the date.

Polish Sausage and Pasta Casserole

Preparation time: 5 minutes | Cooking time: 1 hour

Servings: 2

Ingredients:

- 4 cups uncooked penne pasta
- 1 1/2 pounds Polish smoked sausage (cut into 1/2" slices)
- 1 (16 ounce) jar sauerkraut (rinsed, well-drained)
- 2 (10 3/4 ounce) cans of condensed cream of mushroom soup, undiluted
- 1 1/3 cups 2% milk
- 3 cups Swiss cheese (shredded, divided)
- 2 tbsp Dijon mustard
- 4 green onions (chopped)
- 4 garlic cloves (peeled, minced)

Directions:

1. Preheat the main oven to 350 F.
2. Cook the penne pasta according to the package directions; drain and transfer to a large mixing bowl.
3. Stir in the slices of sausage, sauerkraut, cream of mushroom soup, milk, 2 cups of Swiss cheese, Dijon mustard, onions, and garlic.
4. Spoon the mixture into 2 (8") square greased casserole dishes and sprinkle with the remaining 1 cup of cheese.
5. Bake, uncovered, in the preheated oven until it is golden brown and bubbly, this will take between 45-50 minutes.
6. To freeze-dry the Polish Sausage and Pasta Casserole. First, spoon them onto the trays, and then spread it out to a thickness of approximately half an inch. Place the trays into the freeze dryer's rack.

7. Put in the insulating pad, and close and secure the door. Push start.

8. After it's done, extract the trays from the freeze dryer. Put it in a Mylar bag with an oxygen-absorbing packet, seal it, and label it with the date.

Rosemary Shrimp

Preparation time: 5 minutes | Cooking time: 45 minutes

Servings: 3

Ingredients:

- 6 tbsp freshly squeezed lemon juice
- 8 tbsp olive oil
- 2 tsp salt
- 1/2 tsp ground black pepper
- 1/2 tsp red pepper flakes
- 6 cloves of garlic (peeled, minced)
- 2 (6") sprigs of rosemary (stems discarded, finely chopped)
- 40 jumbo shrimp (peeled, deveined)
- Nonstick cooking spray
- Wedges of lemon

Directions:

1. In a zip lock bag, combine the lemon juice, oil, salt, pepper, red pepper flakes, garlic, and rosemary.

2. Add the shrimp to the bag, seal and gently shake to coat evenly.

3. Transfer to the fridge to marinate for half an hour, while occasionally turning the bag.

4. When you are ready to cook, run the zip lock bag under warm running water until the shrimp are thawed.

5. Remove the shrimp from the bag and grill, for a couple of minutes on each side, until pink.

6. Serve with wedges of lemon and enjoy.

7. To freeze-dry the shrimps. First, put them onto the trays, and then spread it out to a thickness of approximately half an inch. Place the trays into the freeze dryer's rack.

8. Put in the insulating pad, and close and secure the door. Push start.

9. After it's done, extract the trays from the freeze dryer. Put it in a Mylar bag with an oxygen-absorbing packet, seal it, and label it with the date.

★ ★ ★ ★ ★

Shrimp Stir Fry

Preparation time: 5 minutes | Cooking time: 25 minutes

Servings: 2

Ingredients:

- 1/3 cup soy sauce
- 1 tbsp brown sugar
- 1 tsp garlic (peeled, minced)
- 1/2 tsp ground ginger
- Pinch of crushed red pepper flakes
- 1-pound raw shrimp (peeled)
- 2 cups broccoli florets
- 1 red bell pepper (sliced)
- 1 1/2 cups snow peas
- 1 cup carrots (trimmed, shredded)
- 1 tbsp cornstarch + 1 tbsp water (optional)

Directions:

1. For the freezer: In freezer-safe, one-gallon Ziplock bag combine the soy sauce with the brown sugar, garlic, ginger,

and red pepper flakes. Seal and gently shake to combine.

2. Add the shrimp to the bottom of the Ziplock bag along with the broccoli florets, peppers, peas, and carrots. Re-seal the bag and gently squeezed to expel as much air as you can. Lay the bag flat in the freezer and freeze.

3. When you are ready to serve, over moderate heat, heat a large frying pan or skillet and drizzle with oil.

4. Add the stir-fry to the pan and cook until the veggies are tender and the shrimp are pink, this will take between 10-15 minutes.

5. If the stir-fry needs thickening, combine the cornstarch with the water in a bowl, stir to create a slurry and stir into the pan, stir-frying for an addition 2-3 minutes, to allow the sauce to thicken.

6. Remove the pan from the heat and serve at once with boiled rice, fried rice or noodles.

7. To freeze-dry the dish. First, spoon it onto the trays, and then spread it out to a thickness of approximately half an inch. Place the trays into the freeze dryer's rack.

8. Put in the insulating pad, and close and secure the door. Push start.

9. After it's done, extract the trays from the freeze dryer. Put it in a Mylar bag with an oxygen-absorbing packet, seal it, and label it with the date.

Slow Cooker Pepper Steak

Preparation time: 5 minutes | Cooking time: 6 hours

Servings: 4

Ingredients:

- 1 (3 pound) beef top round roast

- 1 large onion (peeled, halved, sliced)
- 1 large green pepper (cut into 1/2" strips)
- 1 large sweet red pepper (cut into 1/2" strips)
- 1 cup water
- 4 garlic cloves (peeled, minced)
- 1/3 cup cornstarch
- 1/2 cup reduced-sodium soy sauce
- 2 tsp sugar
- 2 tsp ground ginger
- 8 cups hot cooked brown rice

Directions:

1. Add the roast beef, onion, green and red peppers to a slow cooker.
2. Add the water along with the garlic and covered, cook for 6-8 hours on low, until the meat is bite-tender.
3. Remove the meat to a chopping board.
4. Transfer the veggies along with the cooking juices to a large pan and bring to boil.
5. In a small-size bowl, combine the cornstarch with the soy sauce, sugar and ginger until silky smooth. Stir into the veggie mixture.
6. Return to boil, while continually stirring and cook for 1-2 minutes, until thickened.
7. Slice the beef and gently stir it into the sauce, until heated through.
8. Serve and enjoy with rice.
9. To freeze-dry the steaks. First, put them onto the trays, and then spread it out to a thickness of approximately half an inch. Place the trays into the freeze dryer's rack.
10. Put in the insulating pad, and close and secure the door. Push start.
11. After it's done, extract the trays from the freeze dryer. Put it in a Mylar bag with an oxygen-absorbing packet, seal it, and

label it with the date.

Speedy Freezer Chicken Curry

Preparation time: 5 minutes |Cooking time: 45 minutes

Servings: 2

Ingredients:

- 2 pounds boneless skinless chicken breasts (rinsed, trimmed, cut into bite-size pieces)
- Salt and pepper
- 1/3 cup butter
- 2/3 cups onion (peeled, chopped)
- 1 tbsp + 1 tsp curry powder
- 2 tsp ginger (minced)
- 2 tsp garlic (minced)
- 2 tsp sugar
- 2 tsp chicken bouillon powder
- 2/3 tsp salt
- 1/3 cup all-purpose flour
- 1 1/3 cups water
- 1 1/3 cups milk
- 2 tsp freshly squeezed lemon juice

Directions:

1. For the freezer: Lightly season the chicken with salt and pepper.
2. Over moderate heat, in a large frying pan, cook the chicken for 10 minutes, until no pink remains. Remove from the heat and then set aside to cool.
3. While the chicken is cooling, over moderate heat, in a large pan melt the butter.

4. Add the onions and then cook while stirring until softened for approximately 5 minutes.

5. Add the curry powder followed by the ginger, garlic, sugar, chicken bouillon powder, and salt, and cook while stirring for a couple of minutes.

6. Add the flour and cook while stirring for 2 minutes, to create a paste-like consistency.

7. A little at a time, add the water along with the milk and cook while continually stirring, until thickened.

8. Whisk in the fresh lemon juice and allow the sauce to cool.

9. Evenly spread the sauce over the chicken, serve.

10. To freeze-dry the chicken curry. First, put it onto the tray, and then spread it out to a thickness of approximately half an inch. Place the tray into the freeze dryer's rack.

11. Put in the insulating pad, and close and secure the door. Push start.

12. After it's done, extract the tray from the freeze dryer. Put it in a Mylar bag with an oxygen-absorbing packet, seal it, and label it with the date.

★ ★ ★ ★ ★

Sweet n' Spicy Asian Meatballs

Preparation time: 5 minutes | Cooking time: 3 hours

Servings: 2

Ingredients:

- 1 egg (beaten)
- 1/2 medium onion (peeled, finely chopped)
- 1/3 cup sliced water chestnuts (diced)
- 3 tbsp fresh cilantro (minced)
- 1 jalapeno pepper (deseeded, finely chopped)
- 3 tbsp reduced-sodium soy sauce

- 4 garlic cloves (peeled, minced)
- 1 tbsp fresh ginger root (minced)
- 2/3 cup panko breadcrumbs
- 2 pounds ground pork Sauce:
- 2 cups ready-made sweet and sour sauce
- 1/4 cup BBQ sauce, of choice
- 1/4 cup store-bought duck sauce
- 2 tbsp chicken broth
- 1 tbsp fresh cilantro (minced)
- 1 tbsp reduced-sodium soy sauce
- 2 garlic cloves (peeled, minced)
- 1 1/2 tsp fresh gingerroot (minced)
- Green onions (thinly sliced)

Directions:

1. Preheat the main oven to 375 degrees F.
2. In a bowl, combine the first eight ingredients (egg, onion, chestnuts, cilantro, jalapeno pepper, soy sauce, garlic, and ginger root).
3. Stir in the breadcrumbs and add the ground pork, mixing thoroughly but lightly.
4. Shape the mixture into a 1 1/4" balls and arrange in a single layer on a greased rack set in a 15x10x1" baking pan and bake in the oven for 18-20 minutes, until gently browned.
5. Transfer the meatballs to a slow cooker of 4-5 quart capacity.
6. In a bowl, prepare the sauce, by mixing the sweet and sour sauce with the BBQ sauce, duck sauce, chicken broth, cilantro, soy sauce, garlic cloves, and the ginger root. Mix to combine and pour evenly over the meatballs.
7. Cook on low, while covered for 3-4 hours until sufficiently cooked through.
8. If cooking immediately, garnish with sliced green onions and serve.
9. To freeze-dry the meatballs. First, put them onto the trays, and

then spread it out to a thickness of approximately half an inch. Place the trays into the freeze dryer's rack.

10. Put in the insulating pad, and close and secure the door. Push start.

11. After it's done, extract the trays from the freeze dryer. Put it in a Mylar bag with an oxygen-absorbing packet, seal it, and label it with the date.

Tuscan Chicken Pasta Bake

Preparation time: 5 minutes | Cooking time: 55 minutes

Servings: 2

Ingredients:

- Nonstick spray
- 1 (13 1/4 ounce) package whole wheat penne pasta
- 1 (7 ounce) jar julienne-cut sun-dried tomatoes in oil (drained, oil reserved, patted dry)
- 1 1/4 pounds boneless skinless chicken breasts (cut into bite-sized pieces)
- 1 small onion (peeled, diced)
- 1 clove garlic (peeled, minced)
- 5 ounces fresh baby kale
- 3 ounces reduced-fat cream cheese
- 1 cup whole milk
- 1/2 cup Parmesan cheese (freshly grated)
- 1 cup Mozzarella cheese (shredded)

Directions:

1. Spritz a 9x13" baking dish with nonstick baking spray. If enjoying immediately, rather than freezing, preheat the main oven to 350 degrees F.

2. Bring a pan of salted water to boil and cook the penne until al dente. Drain.

3. In the meantime, in a large deep frying pan, heat 1 tbsp of the reserved sun-dried tomatoes in oil and add the chicken along with the onions.

4. Cook until the chicken is sufficiently cooked through and the onions translucent while occasionally stirring for approximately 5 minutes.

5. Add the garlic and cook for 60 seconds, until fragrant.

6. Add the kale along with the sun-dried tomatoes and while frequently stirring, cook until the kale is wilted.

7. Add the cream cheese, milk, and grated Parmesan cheese, stirring well to incorporate.

8. Cook until the cream cheese is entirely melted and combined.

9. Add the drained penne pasta and gently stir to coat evenly.

10. Transfer the mixture into the baking dish and top with shredded Mozzarella cheese.

11. If immediately serving, place the dish in the preheated oven and cook for half an hour, until the cheese is entirely melted.

12. To freeze-dry the chicken pasta dish. First, put it onto the trays, and then spread it out to a thickness of approximately half an inch. Place the trays into the freeze dryer's rack.

13. Put in the insulating pad, and close and secure the door. Push start.

14. After it's done, extract the trays from the freeze dryer. Put it in a Mylar bag with an oxygen-absorbing packet, seal it, and label it with the date.

Chicken Cacciatore

Preparation time: 5 minutes | Cooking time: 1 hour

Servings: 5

Ingredients:

- 4 ounces chicken (chopped)
- 1/4 cup all-purpose flour
- Salt and black pepper
- 2 tbsp olive oil
- 2 tbsp butter
- 1 large-size onion (peeled and chopped)
- 2 ribs of celery (sliced)
- 1 large-size green bell pepper (cut into strips)
- 1/2 pound fresh mushrooms (sliced)
- 2 (14 ounces) cans tomatoes (drained and chopped)
- 1 (6 ounces) can tomato paste
- 1 cup dry red wine
- 1 tsp dried thyme
- 1 tsp dried oregano
- 1 tsp dried rosemary (crushed)
- 1 tsp dried basil
- 3 cloves of garlic (peeled and minced)
- 1 tbsp sugar
- Pasta (cooked, hot, to serve)
- Parmesan cheese (freshly grated, to serve)

Directions:

1. Lightly dust the pieces of chicken with flour and season with salt and black pepper.
2. In a large-size skillet or frying pan, in oil and butter, brown the chicken on all sides over moderate-heat heat. Remove the chicken to a plate.
3. In the same pan, while stirring, cook the onion along with the

celery, pepper, and mushrooms for 5 minutes.

4. Stir in the canned tomatoes followed by the tomato sauce, tomato paste, red wine, thyme, oregano, rosemary, basil, garlic, and sugar. Bring to boil, cover with a lid, then simmer for half an hour.

5. Return the chicken to the pan, and cover with a lid. Next, simmer for 45-60 minutes, until the chicken is cooked through.

6. Serve on a bed of pasta, garnished with freshly grated Parmesan cheese.

7. To freeze-dry the chicken cacciatore. First, put them onto the trays, and then spread it out to a thickness of approximately half an inch. Place the trays into the freeze dryer's rack.

8. Put in the insulating pad, and close and secure the door. Push start.

9. After it's done, extract the trays from the freeze dryer. Put it in a Mylar bag with an oxygen-absorbing packet, seal it, and label it with the date.

Chicken Pot Pie

Preparation time: 5 minutes | Cooking time: 1hour

Servings: 7

Ingredients:

- 2 cups potatoes (peeled and diced)
- 1 3/4 cups carrots (sliced)
- 1 cup butter (cubed)
- 2/3 cup onion (peeled and chopped)
- 1 cup all-purpose flour
- 1 3/4 tsp salt
- 1 tsp dried thyme

- 3/4 tsp pepper
- 1 1/2 cups whole milk
- 3 cups chicken stock
- 4 cups cooked chicken (cubed)
- 1 cup frozen peas
- 1 cup frozen corn kernels
- 4 sheets store-bought refrigerated pie crust

Directions:

1. Add the potatoes along with the carrots to a large pan. Pour in sufficient water to cover and bring to boil. Turn the heat down and cook, while covered for 8-10 minutes, until tender but crisp. Drain.

2. In a large frying pan, over moderate-high heat, heat the butter. Add the onion to the pan and cook while stirring until tender. Stir in the flour along with the salt, thyme, and pepper until incorporated.

3. A little at a time, stir in the milk and chicken stock. Bring the mixture to boil, stirring continually, and cook for 3 minutes, until it thickens.

4. Stir in the chicken followed by the peas, corn kernels, and the potato mixture. Take the pan off the heat.

5. Unroll 2 sheets of pastry and use it to line 2 (9") pie plates. Trim, so the pastry is even with the rims of the dishes.

6. Add the chicken mixture, unroll the remaining 2 sheets of pastry and place them over the filling. Trim, seal and flute the pastry edges. Then, make slits in the top of each pie to allow any steam to escape.

7. Preheat your main oven to 425 degrees F. Next, bake in the oven for 35-40 minutes, until the pie crust browns. Allow the pies to stand for 15 minutes before slicing.

8. To freeze-dry the meal. First, put it onto the trays, and then spread it out to a thickness of approximately half an inch. Place the trays into the freeze dryer's rack.

9. Put in the insulating pad, and close and secure the door. Push start.

10. After it's done, extract the trays from the freeze dryer. Put it in a Mylar bag with an oxygen-absorbing packet, seal it, and label it with the date.

Skillet Garlic Chicken Pasta

Preparation time: 5 minutes | Cooking time: 55 minutes

Servings: 8

Ingredients:

- 1 pound fresh chicken breast (cut into 1" pieces)
- 3 tbsp olive oil (divided)
- 1 tbsp butter
- 1 tsp Italian seasoning
- Salt and black pepper (to taste)
- 1/2 cup onion (peeled and chopped)
- 2 garlic cloves (peeled and minced)
- 2 1/2 cups chicken broth
- 1 (14 ounces) can diced tomatoes (undrained)
- 2 1/2 cup uncooked penne pasta
- 1/4 tsp crushed red pepper flakes
- 1/2 cup half and half
- 1 cup mozzarella cheese (shredded)

Directions:

1. Warm a large skillet over moderately-high heat. Next, add 1 1/2 tbsp of olive oil and butter to the pan.

2. When the butter is melted, add the chicken along with the Italian seasoning, salt, and black pepper. Cook until golden brown, for around 15 minutes.

3. Remove the chicken from the pan and transfer to a plate. Set to one side.

4. Turn the heat down to moderate, then add the remaining oil, followed by the onions. Cook the onions until translucent, for 5-6 minutes. Next, add the garlic and cook for 60 seconds.

5. Pour the chicken broth, and add the diced tomatoes, uncooked pasta, red pepper flakes, and chicken set aside in Step 4. Stir well and bring to boil. Then, cover your pan with a lid and turn the heat down to low. Simmer for 15 minutes, until the pasta is bite-tender.

6. Stir in the half and half. Then, allow to stand for approximately 10 minutes, until the sauce thickens. Serve and enjoy.

7. To freeze-dry the garlic chicken pasta. First, put them onto the trays, and then spread it out to a thickness of approximately half an inch. Place the trays into the freeze dryer's rack.

8. Put in the insulating pad, and close and secure the door. Push start.

9. After it's done, extract the trays from the freeze dryer. Put it in a Mylar bag with an oxygen-absorbing packet, seal it, and label it with the date.

Slow Cooker Italian Turkey and Spinach Bean Stew

Preparation time: 5 minutes | Cooking time: 4 hours

Servings: 2

Ingredients:

- 2 pounds ground turkey
- 1 medium-size onion (peeled)
- 1 (14 1/2 ounces) can great Northern beans (drained and

rinsed)

- 2 celery ribs (diced)
- 3 carrots (diced)
- 6 cloves of garlic (peeled and minced)
- 16 ounces chicken stock
- 2 tbsp cooking sherry
- 1 (14 1/2 ounces) can diced tomatoes
- 1 (6 ounces) can green chilies
- 2 tbsp tomato paste
- 8 ounces spinach (frozen and chopped)
- 2 tbsp Herbes de Provence
- 1 tbsp dried basil
- 2 tsp salt
- 1 tsp chili powder
- 1 bay leaf
- 1/4 cup fresh parsley (minced, to garnish)

Directions:

1. In a large frying pan over moderate-high heat, sauté the turkey cooking until no pink remains. Transfer to a bowl.
2. Puree the onion and add it to the bowl containing the turkey followed by the Northern beans, celery, carrots, and garlic.
3. Next to the bowl, add the chicken stock, sherry, tomatoes, green chilies, tomato paste, spinach, Herbes de Provence, basil, salt, chili powder, and bay leaf. Mix thoroughly to combine.
4. Transfer the mixture to a slow cooker of 5-quart capacity. Cover and on low cook for 8-10 hours or on high for 4-6 hours.
5. Garnish with parsley and serve.
6. To freeze-dry the stew. First, put it onto the tray, and then spread it out to a thickness of approximately half an inch. Place the tray into the freeze dryer's rack.
7. Put in the insulating pad, and close and secure the door. Push start.

8. After it's done, extract the tray from the freeze dryer. Put it in a Mylar bag with an oxygen-absorbing packet, seal it, and label it with the date.

Cheesy Ham and Potato Casserole

Preparation time: 5 minutes | Cooking time: 1 hour

Servings: 4

Ingredients:

- Butter (to grease)
- 2 cans (10 3/4 ounces) condensed cream of celery soup
- 1/2 cup water
- 2 cups sour cream
- 1/2 tsp black pepper
- 2 1/2 cups deli ham (cubed)
- 16 ounces processed cheese (cubed)
- 2 (28 ounces) packages frozen hash brown potatoes

Directions:

1. First, preheat the main oven to 375 degrees F. Grease two 2-quart baking dishes.
2. In your large bowl, stir together the soup, water, sour cream, and black pepper.
3. Stir the ham, cheese, and hash browns into the soup mixture, then divide the mixture evenly between the two prepared baking dishes.
4. Next, cover the dishes with aluminum foil and bake in the oven for 40 minutes. Next, uncover and bake for another 10-15 minutes until bubbling.
5. Allow the casseroles to stand for 10 minutes before serving.
6. To freeze-dry the recipe. First, put it onto the tray, and then

spread it out to a thickness of approximately half an inch. Place the tray into the freeze dryer's rack.

7. Put in the insulating pad, and close and secure the door. Push start.

8. After it's done, extract the tray from the freeze dryer. Put it in a Mylar bag with an oxygen-absorbing packet, seal it, and label it with the date.

Crock Pot Beef Fajitas

Preparation time: 5 minutes |Cooking time: 7 hours

Servings: 2

Ingredients:

- 1 1/2 pounds beef chuck steak (cut into 4 pieces)
- 1 medium-size onion (peeled and diced)
- 1 red bell pepper (diced)
- 1 (15 ounces) can diced tomatoes (drained of juice)
- 1 cup beef broth
- 2 tsp garlic (minced)
- 12 ounces ground chorizo

To serve (optional):

- Warm tortillas
- Freshly squeezed lime juice
- Cilantro (chopped)

Directions:

1. In a bowl, combine the steak pieces with the onion, red bell pepper, tomatoes, beef broth, and garlic.

2. In pinch-size amounts, add the ground chorizo to the mixture and stir gently to incorporate.

3. Transfer to your crockpot and cook on low for 7 hours or high for 4-5 hours.

4. To serve, either from fresh or frozen: Remove from the crockpot, shred the meat, removing and discarding any fat. Return the meat to the crop pot, Drain off any excess liquid, as necessary.

5. Serve with warm tortillas, a squeeze of fresh lime juice and chopped cilantro.

6. To freeze-dry the beef fajitas. First, put it onto the tray, and then spread it out to a thickness of approximately half an inch. Place the tray into the freeze dryer rack.

7. Put in the insulating pad, and close and secure the door. Push start.

8. After it's done, extract the tray from the freeze dryer. Put it in a Mylar bag with an oxygen-absorbing packet, seal it, and label it with the date.

Pork Cassoulet

Preparation time: 5 minutes |Cooking time: 45 minutes

Servings: 4

Ingredients:

- Nonstick cooking spray
- 1 pound pork tenderloin (cubed)
- 1 pound smoked kielbasa sausage (sliced)
- 1 yellow onion (peeled, then cut into wedges)
- 3 carrots (peeled and chopped)
- 4 cloves garlic (peeled and minced)
- 2 (14 1/2 ounces) cans stewed tomatoes (chopped)
- 1 (14 1/2 ounces) can chicken broth
- 3 tsp Herbes de Provence

- 1 1/2 tsp garlic powder
- 1 1/2 tsp dried basil
- 1/2 tsp dried oregano
- 1/4 tsp black pepper
- 4 (15 1/2 ounces) cans great Northern beans (drained, rinsed)
- 3/4 cup dry white wine

Directions:

1. Spritz a Dutch oven with nonstick cooking spray.
2. Place the Dutch oven over moderately high heat, add the pork and sausage and sauté until browned. Drain away any fat from the pan.
3. Next, add the onion and carrots, Fry for 3-4 minutes until softened. Add the garlic and fry for 60 more seconds.
4. Pour in the tomatoes, chicken broth, Herbes de Provence, garlic powder, basil, oregano, and black pepper. Bring then the mixture to a boil before turning down to a simmer for 10 minutes.
5. Add one of the cans of beans to a food processor along with a 1/4 cup white wine and blitz to a puree. Transfer to the Dutch oven and stir until incorporated.
6. Add the remaining white wine and canned beans to the cassoulet and stir to combine. Return the mixture to a boil. Lastly, reduce back down to a simmer, then cook for 10 minutes until the veggies and meat are tender.
7. Serve.
8. To freeze-dry the dish. First, put it onto the tray, and then spread it out to a thickness of approximately half an inch. Place the tray into the freeze dryer rack.
9. Put in the insulating pad, and close and secure the door. Push start.
10. After it's done, extract the tray from the freeze dryer. Put it in a Mylar bag with an oxygen-absorbing packet, seal it, and label it with the date.

Slow-Cooked Brazilian Pork and Black Bean Stew

Preparation time: 5 minutes | Cooking time: 7 hours

Servings: 2

Ingredients:

- 1 1/2 cups dried black beans (rinsed)
- 1 pound country-style, boneless pork ribs
- 1 pound smoked kielbasa sausage (sliced)
- 1 smoked ham hock
- 12 ounces cooked chorizo (sliced)
- 3 cloves garlic (peeled and minced)
- 1 yellow onion (peeled, chopped)
- 2 bay leaves
- 3/4 tsp salt
- 1/2 tsp black pepper
- 5 cups water

Directions:

1. Soak the beans according to the packet instructions. Drain, rinse and discard the soaking water.
2. Add the soaked beans to a slow cooker along with the pork ribs, sausage, ham hock, chorizo, garlic, onion, bay leaves, salt, and black pepper. Stir gently to combine.
3. Pour in the water. Cover with the lid and cook for 7-9 hours on low heat until the meat is tender.
4. Take the ham hock and pork ribs out of the slow cooker and allow to cool a little. Next, pick the meat from the bones, set the meat to one side, and discard the bones. Using 2 forks, shred the meat. Then, return to the slow cooker.

5. Discard the bay leaves and stir the stew before serving.

6. To freeze-dry the stew. First, put it onto the tray, and then spread it out to a thickness of approximately half an inch. Place the tray into the freeze dryer rack.

7. Put in the insulating pad, and close and secure the door. Push start.

8. After it's done, extract the tray from the freeze dryer. Put it in a Mylar bag with an oxygen-absorbing packet, seal it, and label it with the date.

Sweet 'n Sour Pork

Preparation time: 5 minutes | Cooking time: 25 minutes

Servings: 5

Ingredients:

- 1/2 cup unsweetened pineapple juice
- 1 tbsp cornstarch
- 1/2 cup BBQ sauce
- 1 cup whole-berry cranberry sauce
- 1 tbsp canola oil
- 1 1/2 cups pork tenderloin (cubed)
- 1/2 tsp salt
- 1/4 tsp black pepper
- 3/4 cup canned pineapple tidbits
- 1 green bell pepper (seeded, sliced thinly)

Directions:

1. In a bowl, stir together the pineapple juice and cornstarch until combined. Add the BBQ sauce and cranberry sauce and stir again. Set aside for a moment.

2. Warm the oil in your skillet over moderately high heat, add

the pork and sauté until browned all over, for approximately 3 minutes—season with salt and black pepper. Take the meat out of the skillet and keep warm.

3. Add the pineapple and bell pepper to the skillet and fry for a couple of minutes. Pour in the set-aside sauce and stir to combine. Cook the mixture for 2-3 minutes until thickened.

4. Return the pork to the skillet and cook until heated through. Serve.

5. To freeze-dry the dish. First, put it onto the tray, and then spread it out to a thickness of approximately half an inch. Place the tray into the freeze dryer rack.

6. Put in the insulating pad, and close and secure the door. Push start.

7. After it's done, extract the tray from the freeze dryer. Put it in a Mylar bag with an oxygen-absorbing packet, seal it, and label it with the date.

Crab Cakes

Preparation time: 5 minutes | Cooking time: 30 minutes

Servings: 2

Ingredients:

- 2 tbsp olive oil
- 2 tbsp celery (diced)
- 2 tbsp yellow onion (diced)
- 2 tbsp red bell pepper (diced)
- Salt and black pepper
- 1/2 cup mayonnaise
- 1 tsp Dijon mustard
- 1 tsp Worcestershire sauce
- 1 egg (lightly beaten)

- 1/2 tsp Old Bay seasoning
- 1 tsp dried parsley
- 1/2 tsp garlic powder
- 2 (6 ounces) cans crabmeat (drained)
- 1/2 cup + extra panko breadcrumbs
- 1 tbsp unsalted butter
- Lemon wedges (to serve)
- Salad (to serve)

Directions:

1. Warm 1 tbsp of oil in a skillet over moderately high heat. Add the celery, onion, and red bell pepper, sauté for 2-3 minutes until softened. Season then to taste with salt and black pepper. Take off the heat and allow to cool.
2. In your bowl, combine the mayonnaise, Worcestershire sauce, egg, Old Bay seasoning, parsley, and garlic powder. Stir in the sautéed veggies.
3. Next, fold in the crabmeat and 1/2 cup breadcrumbs. Cover the bowl with plastic wrap and chill for half an hour.
4. Form the mixture into 4 equally-sized patties.
5. Add breadcrumbs to a shallow dish and dip each patty in the breadcrumbs to coat lightly.
6. Melt together the remaining oil and butter in a pan over moderate heat. Add the patties to the pan and cook for 3-4 minutes on each side.
7. Lastly, serve hot with lemon wedges on the side and salad.
8. To freeze-dry the crab cakes. First, put them onto the trays, and then spread it out to a thickness of approximately half an inch. Place the trays into the freeze dryer's rack.
9. Put in the insulating pad, and close and secure the door. Push start.
10. After it's done, extract the trays from the freeze dryer. Put it in a Mylar bag with an oxygen-absorbing packet, seal it, and label it with the date.

Fish Sticks

Preparation time: 5 minutes | Cooking time: 20 minutes

Servings: 2

Ingredients:

- Avocado oil (to grease)
- 1 pound frozen cod filets (defrosted)
- 1 cup all-purpose flour
- 4 large-size eggs (beaten)
- 2 1/2 cups seasoned panko breadcrumbs
- 1 tsp sea salt

Directions:

1. First, preheat the main oven to 400 degrees F.
2. Prepare 2 roasting pans. Place a wire cooking rack inside each pan. Lightly grease the racks with avocado oil.
3. Partially defrost the fish, before slicing the fish into 24-30 (1/2" wide by 3" long) strips. Pat the strip dry with kitchen paper towels.
4. Add the flour to a shallow bowl, and the beaten egg to a second shallow bowl and then the breadcrumbs to a third shallow bowl.
5. In batches, dredge the fish sticks, first in the flour, second in the egg, and third in the breadcrumbs. Make sure that the sticks are evenly coated.
6. Place the breaded fish stick on top of the wire racks. Season with salt.
7. Bake the fish sticks in the oven for 8 minutes. Turn them over and bake on the other side for 6 minutes before transferring them to the broiler to brown for approximately 60 seconds. Serve hot.

8. To freeze-dry the fish sticks. First, put them onto the trays, and then spread it out to a thickness of approximately half an inch. Place the trays into the freeze dryer's rack.

9. Put in the insulating pad, and close and secure the door. Push start.

10. After it's done, extract the trays from the freeze dryer. Put them in a Mylar bag with an oxygen-absorbing packet, seal it, and label it with the date.

Mediterranean Shrimp

Preparation time: 5 minutes | Cooking time: 20 minutes

Servings: 5

Ingredients:

- 1/4 cup olive oil
- 3 cloves garlic (peeled and minced)
- 3 tbsp fresh lemon juice
- 1/4 tsp black pepper
- 1 tsp salt
- 1/2 tsp dried oregano
- 1/8 tsp red pepper flakes
- 1/2 tsp dried basil
- 1 pound large, fresh shrimp (peeled, then deveined)
- Small handful fresh parsley (chopped)
- 3 tbsp feta cheese (crumbled) Lemon wedges

Directions:

1. In your bowl, combine the olive oil, minced garlic, lemon juice, black pepper, salt, oregano, red pepper flakes, and dried basil to create a marinade.

2. Add the shrimp to the marinade, toss to combine, and chill for

half an hour.

3. Preheat your oven's broiler and cover a baking sheet with kitchen foil.

4. Take the shrimp out of the marinade and arrange on the baking sheet. Place the shrimp under the broiler and cook for 2 minutes on each side or until cooked through.

5. Serve the shrimp garnished with fresh parsley, crumbled feta cheese, and lemon wedges.

6. To freeze-dry the shrimp. First, put it onto the tray, and then spread it out to a thickness of approximately half an inch. Place the tray into the freeze dryer rack.

7. Put in the insulating pad, and close and secure the door. Push start.

8. After it's done, extract the tray from the freeze dryer. Put it in a Mylar bag with an oxygen-absorbing packet, seal it, and label it with the date.

Pecan-Crusted Snapper

Preparation time: 5 minutes | Cooking time: 20 minutes

Servings: 2

Ingredients:

- 1/2 cup dried breadcrumbs
- 1/2 tsp salt
- 2 tbsp pecans (finely chopped)
- 1/4 tsp black pepper
- 1/4 tsp powdered garlic
- 1/2 tsp hot sauce
- 1/2 cup buttermilk
- 3 tbsp all-purpose flour
- 4 (6 ounces) snapper fillets

- 1 tbsp canola oil

Directions:

1. In your shallow dish, combine the breadcrumbs, salt, pecans, black pepper, and garlic.
2. To a second shallow dish, add hot sauce and buttermilk – stir to combine.
3. Next, add the flour to a third shallow dish.
4. Dredge each fish fillet in the flour firstly, then the buttermilk, and finally the breadcrumbs.
5. Warm half of the oil in your skillet over moderately high heat. Add two pieces of the fish to the pan and sauté for 3 minutes on each side until cooked through.
6. Repeat with the remaining oil and fish.
7. To freeze-dry the dish. First, put it onto the tray, and then spread it out to a thickness of approximately half an inch. Place the tray into the freeze dryer rack.
8. Put in the insulating pad, and close and secure the door. Push start.
9. After it's done, extract the tray from the freeze dryer. Put it in a Mylar bag with an oxygen-absorbing packet, seal it, and label it with the date.

Greek Whole Grain Pasta Bake

Preparation time: 5 minutes | Cooking time: 45 minutes

Servings: 5

Ingredients:

- 3 1/3 cups uncooked whole grain spiral pasta
- 1 (29 ounces) can tomato sauce
- 4 cups cooked chicken breast (cubed)

- 1 (14 1/2 ounces) can diced tomatoes (drained)
- 1 (10 ounces) package frozen spinach, chopped (thawed)
- 5 1/2 ounces sliced olives
- 1/4 cup green pepper (chopped)
- 1/4 cup red onion (peeled and thinly sliced)
- 1 tsp dried oregano
- 1 tsp dried basil
- Nonstick cooking spray
- 1 cup mozzarella cheese (shredded)
- 1/2 cup feta cheese (crumbled)
- Fresh oregano (chopped, to garnish)

Directions:

1. Cook the pasta firstly according to the package instructions and until al dente, drain well.
2. In a bowl, combine the drained pasta with the tomato sauce, cubed chicken, diced tomatoes, spinach, olives, green pepper, red onion, oregano, and basil.
3. Spritz a 13x9" casserole with nonstick cooking spray.
4. Transfer the pasta mixture to the prepared dish. Then, scatter the shredded cheese over the top and uncovered, bake at 400 degrees F, for 25-30 minutes, until heated through and the cheese melted.
5. Season with chopped oregano and enjoy.
6. To freeze-dry the pasta dish. First, put it onto the trays, and then spread it out to a thickness of approximately half an inch. Place the trays into the freeze dryer's rack.
7. Put in the insulating pad, and close and secure the door. Push start.
8. After it's done, extract the trays from the freeze dryer. Put it in a Mylar bag with an oxygen-absorbing packet, seal it, and label it with the date.

Green Chili Quiche

Preparation time: 5 minutes | Cooking time: 1hour

Servings: 2

Ingredients:

- 1 (9") prepared single crust pie shell
- 2 tbsp cornmeal
- 1 1/2 cups Monterey Jack cheese (shredded)
- 1 cup Cheddar cheese (shredded)
- 1 (4 ounces) can chopped green chilies
- 3 large-size eggs
- 3/4 cup sour cream
- 1 tbsp fresh cilantro (minced)
- 2-4 drops hot pepper sauce (as needed)

Directions:

1. First, line the pie shell with a double layer of heavy-duty aluminum foil. Then, bake at 450 degrees F. for 8 minutes. Take the foil off, then bake for an additional 5 minutes. Set aside to cool on a wire baking rack and turn the heat down to 350 degrees F.
2. Scatter the cornmeal over the crust.
3. In a small-size bowl, combine the Monterey Jack cheese with the Cheddar cheese. Set 1/2 cup aside for the topping.
4. Add the green chilies to the remaining cheese mixture, and sprinkle onto the crust.
5. In a small-size bowl, whisk the eggs with the sour cream, cilantro, and hot sauce.
6. Then, pour the mixture into the crust and scatter with the cheese mixture set aside in Step 3.
7. Bake in the oven until springy to the touch, this will take 35-40 minutes. Allow to stand for 4-5 minutes before slicing.
8. To freeze-dry the quiche dish. First, put it onto the tray, and

then spread it out to a thickness of approximately half an inch. Place the tray into the freeze dryer rack.

9. Put in the insulating pad, and close and secure the door. Push start.

10. After it's done, extract the tray from the freeze dryer. Put it in a Mylar bag with an oxygen-absorbing packet, seal it, and label it with the date.

★ ★ ★ ★ ★

Tofu Pineapple Stir Fry

Preparation time: 5 minutes | Cooking time: 30 minutes

Servings: 2

Ingredients:

Sauce:

- 1/4 cup liquid aminos
- 3 garlic cloves (peeled and minced)
- 2 tbsp fresh ginger (peeled and grated)
- 2 tbsp pure maple syrup
- 2 tbsp unseasoned rice vinegar
- 2 tbsp fresh lime juice
- 2 tbsp avocado oil

Stir Fry:

- 2 tsp oil
- 1 (14 ounces) block tofu (cut into bite-size cubes)
- 1 green bell pepper (chopped)
- 1 red bell pepper (chopped)
- 2 cups frozen, canned or fresh pineapple chunks
- 1 cup green beans (chopped)
- 1/2 yellow onion (peeled and chopped)

Directions:

1. In a bowl, combine the liquid aminos with the minced garlic, fresh ginger, maple syrup, rice vinegar, fresh lime juice, and avocado oil, whisk until incorporated. If making ahead to freeze rather than enjoying immediately, follow freezer instructions, otherwise continue with Steps 2-4.

2. Add the oil to a pan and over moderate-high heat, cook the tofu until golden brown. This step will take 7-9 minutes in total, and you will need to stir every 1-2 minutes.

3. Next, add the bell peppers, pineapple chunks, green beans, and yellow onion to a large frying pan and cook while stirring continually over moderate heat until tender, for 2-3 minutes.

4. Add the sauce to the pan, stir to combine, heat through for 2-3 minutes, and serve.

5. To freeze-dry the recipe. First, put it onto the trays, and then spread it out to a thickness of approximately half an inch. Place the tray into the freeze dryer rack.

6. Put in the insulating pad, and close and secure the door. Push start.

7. After it's done, extract the tray from the freeze dryer. Put it in a Mylar bag with an oxygen-absorbing packet, seal it, and label it with the date.

Tomato and Basil Soup

Preparation time: 5 minutes | Cooking time: 10 minutes

Servings: 2

Ingredients:

- 1/4 cup tomato powder
- 1/3 cup instant dried milk powder
- 2 tbsp bouillon granules

- 1 tsp dried basil
- 1/8 tsp of garlic powder
- 1/8 Tsp onion powder
- 1/8 teaspoon freshly ground black pepper
- 1/4 tsp salt
- 1 3/4 cups boiling water (divided)

Directions:

1. Toss in the tomato powder, instant milk powder, bouillon powders, dried basil, garlic powder and onion powder.
2. Mix the ingredients together by stirring or massaging them until they are well combined.
3. Mix the ingredients in a 2+ cup mug or bowl. Stir in half the boiling water and mix well until it is all incorporated. Stir in the remaining boiling water.
4. Cover with a towel and let it rest for between 8-10 minutes.
5. To freeze-dry the soup. First, put it onto the tray, and then spread it out to a thickness of approximately half an inch. Place the tray into the freeze dryer rack.
6. Put in the insulating pad, and close and secure the door. Push start.
7. After it's done, extract the tray from the freeze dryer. Put it in a Mylar bag with an oxygen-absorbing packet, seal it, and label it with the date.

★ ★ ★ ★ ★

Banana Bread Instant Oatmeal

Preparation time: 5 minutes | Cooking time: 5 minutes

Servings: 4

Ingredients:

- 1/2 cup instant oatmeal

- 3 tbsp frozen-dried banana (chopped).
- 1/8 tsp vanilla bean
- 1 tbsp walnuts (chopped)
- 2 tsp sugar
- 3/4 cup milk (boiling)
- Walnuts (optional, chopped, to serve)

Directions:

1. Combine the instant oatmeal, bananas, vanilla bean and walnuts in a Mason jar.
2. The jar can be kept in a dry, cool place for up to 28 day.
3. Pour the boiling water or milk over the oatmeal and stir it well. Mix well and let it sit for three minutes to rehydrate.
4. Add extra chopped walnuts to your dish and enjoy.
5. To freeze-dry the oatmeal. First, put them onto the trays, and then spread it out to a thickness of approximately half an inch. Place the trays into the freeze dryer's rack.
6. Put in the insulating pad, and close and secure the door. Push start.
7. After it's done, extract the trays from the freeze dryer. Put it in a Mylar bag with an oxygen-absorbing packet, seal it, and label it with the date.

Beef 'n Bean Stew in a Jar

Preparation time: 5 minutes | Cooking time: 15 minutes

Servings: 2

Ingredients:

- 1 cup quick-cook black beans
- 1 cup freeze-dried diced beef
- 2 tbsp powdered beef bouillon

- 2 tbsp frozen minced onions
- 1 tsp granulated garlic
- 1 tsp thyme
- 2 tbsp tomato powder
- 1 cup dehydrated diced potatoes
- 1 cup freeze-dried mixed vegetables
- 1 tsp salt
- 6 cups water

Directions:

1. In a clean 1-quart jar, layer the ingredients according to recipe. To settle the mixture, shake the jar gently.
2. Place a canning lid over the jar. Seal it with a vacuum seal. Add a ring and tighten by hand, taking care to not overtighten.
3. Label, date and store until required.
4. Once you're ready to cook, take off the lid and discard.
5. Transfer the contents of the jar to a large saucepan.
6. Bring 6 cups water into the pot. Heat on medium to high heat until it boils.
7. Reduce the heat and let it simmer for 20 minutes. Serve and enjoy.
8. To freeze-dry the stew. First, put it onto the trays, and then spread it out to a thickness of approximately half an inch. Place the trays into the freeze dryer's rack.
9. Put in the insulating pad, and close and secure the door. Push start.
10. After it's done, extract the trays from the freeze dryer. Put it in a Mylar bag with an oxygen-absorbing packet, seal it, and label it with the date.

★ ★ ★ ★ ★

Breakfast Scramble with Spinach and Sun-dried Peppers

Preparation time: 5 minutes | Cooking time: 10 minutes

Servings: 4

Ingredients:

- 3/4 cup whole egg crystals
- 1/2 teaspoon powdered garlic powder
- 1/2 tbsp salt
- 1/2 tsp ground black pepper
- 1/2 cup sun-dried tomatoes (chopped)
- 1/2 cup dehydrated spinach
- 1 1/4 cups water
- 1 tbsp olive oil

Directions:

1. At home, combine the whole egg crystals with the garlic powder and salt. Add the water outside your home to the Ziplock bag. Mix the ingredients together with a fork until they are well combined. Allow the spinach to rest for three minutes before putting it on the plate.
2. Heat the oil in a saucepan or pot on low heat. Mix the egg-spinach and pepper mixtures together and use a spoon to scramble the eggs.
3. Serve and enjoy.
4. To freeze-dry the dish. First, put it onto the tray, and then spread it out to a thickness of approximately half an inch. Place the tray into the freeze dryer rack.
5. Put in the insulating pad, and close and secure the door. Push start.
6. After it's done, extract the tray from the freeze dryer. Put it in a Mylar bag with an oxygen-absorbing packet, seal it, and label it with the date.

Backpacker's Chocolate and Berry Bark

Preparation time: 5 minutes | Cooking time: 25 minutes

Servings: 5

Ingredients:

- 1 pound semi-sweet or dark chocolate (chopped)
- 1 cup freeze-dried strawberries (divided)
- 1 cup crisp rice cereal
- 1/2 cup mini white chocolate chips

Directions:

1. Using parchment paper, line a cookie sheet and put it aside.
2. In a suitable bowl, microwave your choice of chocolate on high in 25-second increments, stirring between increments until melted and smooth. Using a wooden spoon, fold in ½ cup of the freeze-dried strawberries, along with the rice cereal until all of the cereal is coated.
3. With a spatula, spread the mixture as thinly as possible onto the prepared cookie sheet.
4. Before the melted chocolate starts to harden, and while working very quickly, scatter over the remaining strawberries and mini white chocolate chips. Press down gently to adhere.
5. To freeze-dry the Backpacker's Chocolate and Berry Bark. First, put them onto the trays, and then spread it out to a thickness of approximately half an inch. Place the trays into the freeze dryer's rack.
6. Put in the insulating pad, and close and secure the door. Push start.
7. After it's done, extract the trays from the freeze dryer. Put it in a Mylar bag with an oxygen-absorbing packet, seal it, and label it with the date.

Chocolate-Covered Strawberry Trail Mix

Preparation time: 5 minutes | Cooking time: 15 minutes

Servings: 2

Ingredients:

- 3/4 cup roasted almonds
- 3/4 cup roasted cashews
- 3/4 cup roasted sunflower seeds
- 1 cup freeze-dried strawberries
- 2/3 cup dark chocolate chunks

Directions:

1. In a large bowl, combine the almonds with cashews, sunflower seeds, freeze-dried strawberries, and dark chocolate chunks.
2. Transfer the mixture to a large Ziplock bag.
3. To freeze-dry the dish. First, put it onto the trays, and then spread it out to a thickness of approximately half an inch. Place the trays into the freeze dryer's rack.
4. Put in the insulating pad, and close and secure the door. Push start.
5. After it's done, extract the trays from the freeze dryer. Put it in a Mylar bag with an oxygen-absorbing packet, seal it, and label it with the date.

Mocha Peanut Butter and Banana Smoothie

Preparation time: 5 minutes | Cooking time: 5 minutes

Servings: 2

Ingredients:

- 1/3 cup egg white protein powder
- 2 tsp freeze-dried espresso instant coffee
- 1/4 cup freeze-dried bananas (ground)
- 1 individual sachet peanut butter
- 12 ounces water (divided)
- 1 individual sachet powdered hot chocolate mix

Directions:

1. While at home, combine the egg white protein powder with the coffee and ground bananas in a Ziplock bag. Shake the bag gently to distribute evenly.
2. Outside your home, gently massage the peanut butter packet until softened. Pour 6 ounces of water into a sports bottle with a secure screw-top lid.
3. Add the contents from the Ziplock bag along with the hot chocolate mix and coffee to the sports bottle.
4. Screw on the lid and vigorously shake the sports bottle until the smoothie is lump-free, for 35-45 seconds,
5. Add the remaining water to the bottle.
6. Shake the bottle vigorously once more to combine and blend.
7. To freeze-dry the smoothie. First, put the smoothie onto the tray, and then spread it out to a thickness of approximately half an inch. Place the tray into the freeze dryer rack.
8. Put in the insulating pad, and close and secure the door. Push start.
9. After it's done, extract the tray from the freeze dryer. Put it in a Mylar bag with an oxygen-absorbing packet, seal it, and

label it with the date.

White Chocolate Peach and Strawberry Trail Mix

Preparation time: 5 minutes | Cooking time: 4 minutes

Servings: 2

Ingredients:

- 1/2 cup freeze-dried peaches (broken into bite-size pieces)
- 1/2 cup freeze-dried strawberries (broken into bite-size pieces)
- 1/4 cup white chocolate chips
- 1/2 cup granola
- 1/4 cup pretzels (broken into bite-size pieces)
- 1/4 cup roasted peanuts

Directions:

1. In a bowl, combine the peaches with the strawberries, white chocolate chips, granola, pretzels, and roasted peanuts.
2. Transfer the trail mix to a large Ziplock bag and enjoy.
3. To freeze-dry the dish. First, put the dish onto the tray, and then spread it out to a thickness of approximately half an inch. Place the tray into the freeze dryer rack.
4. Put in the insulating pad, and close and secure the door. Push start.
5. After it's done, extract the tray from the freeze dryer. Put it in a Mylar bag with an oxygen-absorbing packet, seal it, and label it with the date.

Yogurt Trail Mix

Preparation time: 5 minutes | Cooking time: 5 minutes

Servings: 4

Ingredients:

- 2 cups freeze-dried, flavor of choice yogurt bites
- 1 cup almonds or peanuts
- 1/2 cup hulled sunflower seeds
- 1/2 cup freeze-dried cherries
- 1 cup freeze-dried strawberry slices

Directions:

1. In a bowl, combine the yogurt bites with the nuts, sunflower seeds, freeze-dried cherries, and strawberry slices.
2. Transfer the mixture to individual Ziplock bags.
3. To freeze-dry the yogurt trail mix. First, put the recipe onto the tray, and then spread it out to a thickness of approximately half an inch. Place the tray into the freeze dryer rack.
4. Put in the insulating pad, and close and secure the door. Push start.
5. After it's done, extract the tray from the freeze dryer. Put it in a Mylar bag with an oxygen-absorbing packet, seal it, and label it with the date.

Lasagna

Preparation time: 5 minutes | Cooking time: 50 minutes

Servings: 2

Ingredients:

- 18 lasagna noodles

- 3 pounds ground beef
- 3 (26 ounce) jars spaghetti sauce
- 2 large eggs (lightly beaten)
- 1 1/2 pounds ricotta cheese
- 1 tbsp dried parsley flakes
- 6 cups part-skim mozzarella cheese (shredded, divided)
- 1 tsp salt
- 1/2 tsp freshly ground black pepper
- 1 cup Parmesan cheese (freshly grated)

Directions:

1. Cook the noodles according to the package directions.
2. In the meantime, in a Dutch oven, cook the beef over moderate heat until no pink remains and drain.
3. Stir in the spaghetti sauce to combine and set aside. In a large mixing bowl, combine the eggs with the ricotta cheese followed by the parsley, 4 1/2 cups of shredded mozzarella cheese, salt, and black pepper.
4. Drain the pasta.
5. Evenly spread 1 cup of meat sauce into each of 2 (13x9") greased casserole dishes.
6. Layer each with three noodles followed by 1 cup ricotta mixture and 1½ cups of meat sauce. Repeat the layers twice. Top with grated Parmesan cheese and the remaining mozzarella.
7. Cover the casserole dish and freeze one lasagna for up to 3 months.
8. Cover and bake the remaining lasagna at 375 degrees F for 45 minutes. Uncover, and bake for an additional 10 minutes or until bubbling. Set aside to stand for several minutes before serving.
9. To freeze-dry the lasagna. First, put the lasagna onto the tray, and then spread it out to a thickness of approximately half an inch. Place the tray into the freeze dryer rack.

10. Put in the insulating pad, and close and secure the door. Push start.

11. After it's done, extract the tray from the freeze dryer. Put it in a Mylar bag with an oxygen-absorbing packet, seal it, and label it with the date.

Baked Potato, Cheese, and Onion Soup

Preparation time: 5 minutes | Cooking time: 6 hours

Servings: 7

Ingredients:

- 5 pounds baking potatoes (cut into 1/2" cubes)
- 1 large onion (peeled, chopped)
- 1/4 cup butter
- 4 garlic cloves (peeled, minced)
- 1 tsp salt
- 1/2 tsp pepper
- 3 (14 1/2 ounce) cans chicken broth
- 1 cup mature Cheddar cheesc (shredded)
- 1 cup half-and-half cream
- 3 tbsp fresh chives (minced)

Toppings (optional):

- Cheddar cheese (shredded)
- Sour cream
- Cooked bacon (crumbled)

Directions:

1. Add the first seven ingredients to a slow cookcr of 6-quart capacity (potatoes, onion, butter, garlic, salt, pepper, and chicken broth).

2. Cover and cook on low for 6-8 hours, until the potatoes, are fork tender.
3. Slightly mash the potatoes to thicken the soup.
4. Add the shredded Cheddar along with the half and half cream, and chives and heat through, stirring until combined.
5. Serve with your favorite toppings.
6. To freeze-dry the soup. First, put the soup onto the trays, and then spread it out to a thickness of approximately half an inch. Place the trays into the freeze dryer rack.
7. Put in the insulating pad, and close and secure the door. Push start.
8. After it's done, extract the trays from the freeze dryer. Put it in a Mylar bag with an oxygen-absorbing packet, seal it, and label it with the date.

Cheats Chicken Pot Pie

Preparation time: 5 minutes | Cooking time: 1 hour

Servings: 2

Ingredients:

- 2 cups cooked chicken (shredded)
- 1 (16 ounce) bag frozen hash browns
- 12 ounces frozen carrot and pea mix
- 1/4 cup onion (peeled, diced small)
- 2 1/2 cups gravy
- Salt and black pepper
- 4 frozen ready-made double pie crusts in foil trays (thawed)

Directions:

1. Preheat the main oven to 350 degrees F.
2. In a bowl, combine the shredded chicken with the hash

browns, veggie mix, onion, and gravy.

3. Season with salt and pepper.

4. Spoon the chicken filling into the bottom crusts and evenly spread.

5. Take the top crust and place it on top of the filling. Spread it to fit and pinch the crusts together to seal.

6. Make a few slash cuts on the top of each pie, to allow the steam to escape.

7. To freeze-dry this recipe. First, put the it onto the trays, and then spread it out to a thickness of approximately half an inch. Place the trays into the freeze dryer rack.

8. Put in the insulating pad, and close and secure the door. Push start.

9. After it's done, extract the trays from the freeze dryer. Put it in a Mylar bag with an oxygen-absorbing packet, seal it, and label it with the date.

Chicken Burrito Casserole

Preparation time: 5 minutes | Cooking time: 3 hours

Servings: 8

Ingredients:

- 6 tbsp butter
- 1 large onion (peeled, chopped)
- 1/4 cup green pepper (chopped)
- 1/2 cup all-purpose flour
- 3 cups chicken broth
- 1 (10 ounce) can diced tomatoes and green chiles (undrained)
- 1 tsp ground cumin
- 1 tsp chili powder
- 1/2 tsp garlic powder

- 1/2 tsp salt
- 2 tbsp jalapeno pepper (chopped)
- 1 (15 ounces) can chili with beans
- 1 (8 ounce) package cream cheese (cut into cubes)
- 8 cups rotisserie chicken (cut into cubes)
- 24 (6") flour tortillas (warm)
- 6 cups s Colby-Monterey Jack cheese (shredded)
- Salsa, store-bought (to serve)

Directions:

1. Over moderate-high heat, in a Dutch oven heat the butter. Add the onion followed by the green pepper and cook while stirring until fork tender.
2. Stir in the flour until incorporated, and gradually stir in the chicken broth. Bring to boil and while stirring cook for an additional 2 minutes.
3. Turn the heat down, and stir in the tomatoes, cumin, chili powder, garlic powder, salt, and jalapeno pepper — Cook for 5 minutes.
4. Add the can of chili along with the cream cheese and stir until entirely melted. Stir in the chicken.
5. Spoon approximately 1/2 cup of the filling across the middle of each of the tortillas. Scatter 1/4 cup Colby-Monterey Jack cheese.
6. Fold the bottom and sides of the tortilla over the filling and carefully roll. Repeat the process until all 24 tortillas are assembled.
7. Transfer each of the filled tortillas in 2 (13x9") lightly greased casserole dishes.
8. To freeze-dry the chicken burrito casserole. First, put the casserole dish onto the freeze dryer trays, and then spread it out to a thickness of approximately half an inch. Place the trays into the freeze dryer rack.
9. Put in the insulating pad, and close and secure the door. Push

start.

10. After it's done, extract the trays from the freeze dryer. Put it in a Mylar bag with an oxygen-absorbing packet, seal it, and label it with the date.

Brown Rice with Corn and Chicken

Preparation time: 5 minutes | Cooking time: 10 minutes

Servings: 2

Ingredients:

- 2/3 cup instant brown rice
- 1 tsp chia seeds
- 1/3 cup frozen chopped chicken
- 1/2 cup freeze-dried corn
- 1/4 cup frozen chopped tomatoes
- 1/4 teaspoon minced dried jalapeno
- 1 tbsp freeze-dried onions
- 1 1/2 tsp powdered Chicken flavor base
- 1 1/2 tsp chili powder
- 1/4 tsp cumin
- 1/4 teaspoon dried Mexican oregano
- 1/2 tsp freeze-dried cilantro
- 1/4 tsp garlic powder
- 1/8 tsp ground black pepper
- 1/4 teaspoon salt (or more according to your taste)
- 1 1/2 cups water

Directions:

1. Mix the brown rice, chia seed, chicken, tomatoes, jalapeno and onions in a Ziplock bag. Add chili powder, cumin.
2. Bring the water to boil outside your home.

3. Place the water in the bag and place it on a plate or bowl. Let the mixture soak in the bag for between 8-10 minutes. After 3-4 minutes, flip the bag upside-down to allow the ingredients to spread evenly.

4. To freeze-dry the rice dish. First, put the rice recipe onto the freeze dryer trays, and then spread it out to a thickness of approximately half an inch. Place the trays into the freeze dryer rack.

5. Put in the insulating pad, and close and secure the door. Push start.

6. After it's done, extract the trays from the freeze dryer. Put it in a Mylar bag with an oxygen-absorbing packet, seal it, and label it with the date. Take the bag out, open it and share.

Chicken Alfredo with Pine Nuts

Preparation time: 5 minutes | Cooking time: 15 minutes

Servings: 5

Ingredients:

- 1 cup angel hair pasta (broken into pieces)
- 1 tsp chia seeds
- 1/4 cup frozen chopped chicken
- 1/4 cup toasted pine nuts
- 1/4 cup frozen chopped mushrooms
- 1 1/2 tsp powdered Chicken flavor base
- 3 Tbsp dry, canned refrigerated, and grated Parmesan Cheese
- 2 tbsp powdered milk
- 2 tbsp cornstarch
- 2 tsp freeze-dried Italian herb blend
- 1/4 tsp garlic powder
- 1/8 teaspoon freshly ground black pepper

- 1/4 teaspoon salt (to taste)
- 1 1/4 cups water

Directions:

1. When you are at home, add the pasta, chia seeds and freeze-dried chopped chicken to a 1 quart Ziplock bag.
2. Cook in the bag outside your home. Bring the water to boil. The boiling water should be poured into the Ziplock bag. Allow the contents to soak for about 8 minutes. After that, turn the bag around to mix the ingredients evenly.
3. Enjoy the contents of the Ziplock bag.
4. Alternatively, you can transfer the contents of the Ziplock bag into a large bowl or mug that is microwave-safe.
5. Place the water in a bowl or mug and heat it in the microwave until it boils.
6. Cover the container and let it rest for at least 4-6 minutes. Stir and allow Alfredo to rest for about a minute before you enjoy.
7. To freeze-dry the chicken alfredo. First, put the dish onto the freeze dryer trays, and then spread it out to a thickness of approximately half an inch. Place the trays into the freeze dryer rack.
8. Put in the insulating pad, and close and secure the door. Push start.
9. 9 After it's done, extract the trays from the freeze dryer. Put it in a Mylar bag with an oxygen-absorbing packet, seal it, and label it with the date.

Raspberry Marshmallow Crème Pie

Preparation time: 5 minutes | Cooking time: 10 minutes

Servings: 4

Ingredients:

- 7 ounces marshmallow crème
- 8 ounces full-fat cream cheese (at room temperature)

- 2 cups raspberry sherbet (softened)
- 2 1/2 cups whipped topping
- 1 (9") graham cracker crust

Directions:

1. Beat together the marshmallow crème and cream cheese until fluffy.
2. Stir in the sherbet, then fold in the whipped topping until incorporated.
3. Spoon the mixture into the pie crust.
4. To freeze-dry the marshmallows. First, put the marshmallows recipe onto the freeze dryer trays, and then spread it out to a thickness of approximately half an inch. Place the trays into the freeze dryer rack.
5. Put in the insulating pad, and close and secure the door. Push start.
6. After it's done, extract the trays from the freeze dryer. Put it in a Mylar bag with an oxygen-absorbing packet, seal it, and label it with the date.

Salted Caramel Blondies

Preparation time: 5 minutes | Cooking time: 35 minutes

Servings: 2

Ingredients:

- Nonstick spray
- 1 cup brown sugar
- 1/2 cup unsalted butter (at room temperature)
- 1 egg
- 1/4 tsp salt
- 1 cup all-purpose flour

- 2 tsp vanilla essence
- 1/4 cup salted caramel sauce

Directions:

1. Preheat the main oven to 350 degrees F. Spritz an 8" square baking tin with nonstick spray.
2. Cream together the sugar and butter until super fluffy and light. Beat in the egg, followed by the salt, flour, and vanilla.
3. Spoon the mixture into the baking tin.
4. Drop blobs of salted caramel on top of the batter and swirl into the mixture using a toothpick or knife.
5. Place in the oven and bake for just over 20 minutes until golden.
6. To freeze-dry the caramel blondies. First, put the dish onto the freeze dryer trays, and then spread it out to a thickness of approximately half an inch. Place the trays into the freeze dryer rack.
7. Put in the insulating pad, and close and secure the door. Push start.
8. After it's done, extract the trays from the freeze dryer. Put it in a Mylar bag with an oxygen-absorbing packet, seal it, and label it with the date.

Zingy Ginger Lemon Layer 'Cake'

Preparation time: 5 minutes | Cooking time: 8 hours

Servings: 5

Ingredients:

- 2 tsp lemon zest (grated)
- 8 ounces full-fat cream cheese (at room temperature)
- 10 ounces lemon curd

- 2 cups heavy whipping cream
- 10 1/2 ounces thin ginger cookies
- 2 tbsp crystallized ginger (chopped)

Directions:

1. Beat the lemon zest into the cream cheese until fluffy.
2. Next, beat in the lemon curd.
3. Beat in the cream gradually, until the mixture can hold soft peaks.
4. Layer 9 ginger cookies in the base of an 8" square dish and spread over 2/3 of a cup of the cream cheese mixture. Repeat these layers 6 more times.
5. Scatter over the chopped crystallized ginger. Chill overnight until firm.
6. To freeze-dry the cake. First, put the dish onto the freeze dryer trays, and then slice the cake and spread it out to a thickness of approximately half an inch. Place the trays into the freeze dryer rack.
7. Put in the insulating pad, and close and secure the door. Push start.
8. After it's done, extract the trays from the freeze dryer. Put it in a Mylar bag with an oxygen-absorbing packet, seal it, and label it with the date

Conclusion

Thank you for taking the time to read this book. Practically any kind of food can be freeze-dried, although some types perform better than others. For example, meat should be cut into smaller pieces to be more suitable for the freeze-drying process, since smaller pieces tend to have better results. Similarly, coffee, soups, and other liquids can also be effectively freeze-dried. In fact, many of the instant coffees that we consume daily are either freeze-dried or spray-dried. Additionally, freeze-dried fruits and vegetables are becoming increasingly popular in stores, as they are considered to be healthier alternatives to dehydrated foods.

It's important to note that freeze-drying machines can be quite expensive, with prices typically ranging between $2000 and $4000. However, if you only plan to freeze-dry a small amount of food each year, you may not need to invest that much money.

Using a deep freezer can be more efficient and speed up the freeze-drying process, as a standard freezer can take weeks to complete the process. It's also important to keep in mind that neither freezing nor freeze-drying methods work well for storing meat, which can be difficult to preserve.

Before freezing food, be sure to clean and dry it thoroughly, removing any dirt or moisture from the items. Additionally, cut all food into uniform chunks to ensure consistency. It's worth noting that yeast-based products, such as bread or cakes, should not be frozen, as they will change color when reconstituted.

The best time to freeze-dry food is when it is cold and has been cooled off. If you are making a complete meal, it's best to freeze-dry it as soon as you are finished cooking it. Then, when rehydrating the food, use a thermometer to ensure that the results are satisfactory.